To my parents who made our sedarim such an intellectual, spiritual, transformative and culinary experience and to all those who have shared sedarim with Marcia and me in our home. Appreciation goes to Cathy Fischgrund of Frances Lincoln for her fine editing skills and attention to detail in producing this beautiful Haggadah. - M.S.

The publishers would like to thank Ilana Tahan of the British Library, Rabbi Frank Dabba Smith and Rabbi Ellen Greenspan for their invaluable support.

The Illuminated Haggadah © Frances Lincoln Limited 1998

Translation of Hebrew text © Union of Liberal and Progressive Synagogues 1996 with adapted or additional translation on pages

8, 9, 15, 16, 17, 21, 28, 29, 38, 44, 46, 55, 56, 59 © Rabbi Dr Michael Shire 1998

All illustrations reproduced by permission of The British Library © British Library Board 1998

First published in Great Britain in 1998 by Frances Lincoln Limited

4 Torriano Mews, Torriano Avenue, London NW5 2RZ

Published in 1998 and distributed in the U.S. by Stewart, Tabori & Chang, a division of U.S. Media Holdings, Inc.

115 West 18th Street, New York, NY 10011

Distributed in Canada by General Publishing Company Ltd.

30 Lesmill Road, Don Mills, Ontario, M3B 2T6, Canada

Library of Congress Cataloging-in-Publication Data

Haggadah. English & Hebrew.

The illuminated Haggadah : featuring medieval illuminations from the haggadah collection of the British Library.

p. cm

ISBN 1-55670-800-9 (hardcover). -- ISBN 1-155670-724-X (pbk.)

1.Haggadot--Texts. 2.Seder--Liturgy--Texts. 3.Judaism--Liturgy--Texts. 4.Haggadah. 5.Haggadah--Illustrations.

6.Illumination of books and manuscripts, Jewish. I.British Library. II.Title

BM674.643.I45 1998

296.4`37--DC21   97-30520

                                              CIP

                                              r97

Designed by Sophie Pelham

Set in Bembo by SX Composing

Hebrew set in Frank Ruehl by JJ Copyprint

Printed in Hong Kong

1 3 5 7 9 8 6 4 2

The ILLUMINATED HAGGADAH

*Featuring Medieval Illuminations from
the Haggadah Collection of the British Library*

STEWART, TABORI & CHANG
NEW YORK

INTRODUCTION

All of us have stories that we repeat through generations. We tell them to our children, and in turn our children tell their children, keeping family memories alive. So it is with the story of the Exodus from Egypt, a moment in history that created the Jewish family.

Since that time the story has been retold over thousands of years and every Jewish family remembers it as the story of our freedom. *The Illuminated Haggadah*, drawing on six priceless manuscripts preserved in the British Library in London, is testimony to this. Centuries old, aglow with glorious illuminations, these manuscripts—both Sephardic (Spanish and Portuguese) and Ashkenazic (Central and Northern European) in origin—are a stirring tribute to the richness and diversity of Jewish history. Their worn pages, specked with wine stains, are a moving reminder of the people who used them generation after generation to celebrate the Feast of Freedom. The miracle of the Israelites' passage from slavery to freedom was as precious to them as it is to us. *The Illuminated Haggadah* connects our celebration with theirs. (Further information about the manuscripts is found in the index at the back of the book.)

The Passover story is in itself an inspiration and it reflects the nature of what a Jewish family represents. It illustrates courage in the face of persecution and despair. It speaks to us of heroes who are ordinary people like each one of us. It points out that miracles are everyday occurrences if only we notice them. And most of all, the story keeps reminding us that God is present in our lives, guiding and protecting us. My commentary offers a personal interpretation of the text, linking the past to a more hopeful future.

In the words of the Haggadah, "In each generation, every person should feel as though they had been freed from Egypt." Only then will we truly cherish freedom. *The Illuminated Haggadah* celebrates the fact that these manuscripts have survived to enrich our lives and the power of this age-old message. Everyone seeks freedom from their own oppression, and if we remain faithful to the Passover story, we realize that we cannot be truly free until all are free.

Rabbi Dr. Michael Shire

PASSOVER AND THE SEDER

The first Passover was celebrated by the Israelites, according to God's command (Ex. 12.1–20), the night before the Exodus. With the creation of the Temple (586 B.C.E.), Passover became a national ceremony: Each year, the priests offered the Paschal sacrifice of a lamb (Pesach) in the Temple and psalms of praise (Hallel) were included in the ritual. After the Temple was destroyed (70 C.E.), the Seder was created as remembrance of the sacrifice. It was conducted in the home as a discussion, study, and eating experience—a unique ritual drawing on Greek and Roman customs of the day.

The Mishnah (200 C.E.) describes the rabbinic Seder on Passover as having four elements: Pesach, Matzah, Maror, and Hallel. New elements were introduced—the idea of hope for a better future and God's redemption for the world—and rabbinic interpretations of biblical passages were added, including the asking of four questions. When all these elements were put together, they comprised an order (in Hebrew, "seder") of fifteen parts.

THE HAGGADAH

The first full account of the Seder night ritual is found in *Seder Rav Amram*, the first Jewish prayer book, edited by Babylonian scholar Rabbi Amram ben Sheshnah in the 9th century C.E. It was only a small part of the prayer book, but the text was approved and is the basis of the Haggadah we use today. The Haggadah, which means "telling," continued to appear in prayer books until the 13th century, when a separate text emerged with additional songs and liturgical poems. Illuminated haggadot flourished during this period until the end of the 15th century when the first haggadot were printed.

THE ARRANGEMENT OF THE SEDER TABLE

On the Seder Plate:
MAROR—sliced or grated horseradish, or the root of lettuce, called chazeret. The maror's bitter taste reminds us of the Israelites' suffering in Egypt.
HAROSET—a sweet combination of apples, nuts, and cinnamon mixed in red wine (a traditional Ashkenazic recipe) to remind us of the mortar the Israelites used to build store houses for the Egyptians. There are different varieties of haroset: Sephardic Jews make it with ingredients such as pistachios, walnuts, pine nuts, coconuts, bananas, dates, or figs.
ZEROA—a roasted lamb shankbone with some meat on it, reminiscent of the Paschal lamb sacrificed in the Temple.
BETZAH—a roasted, boiled egg. The egg is a symbol of birth and represents the Festival Sacrifice (Hagigah) that was offered in Temple times. Roasting the egg has been interpreted as a symbol of mourning for the destruction of the Temple.
KARPAS—parsley, radishes, or celery; Russian and Eastern European communities used boiled potatoes if green vegetables were unavailable before Passover. The karpas is dipped in salt water as a reminder of the Israelites' tears. Iraqi Jews dip it in vinegar.

On the Table:
MATZAH—there are three pieces of matzah on the leader's plate; one is the Afikoman, and the other two are to be eaten before the meal. Matzah is made from water and flour. According to Jewish Law, no longer than eighteen minutes should elapse between mixing and baking the ingredients. This unleavened bread reminds us that when the Israelites fled Egypt, they did not have time to wait for their bread to rise.
SALT WATER—in which to dip the karpas.
WINE—red or white. Everyone is obliged to drink four cups of wine during the Seder. Each participant fills a cup for another, symbolizing freedom—in Greek and Roman times people were considered free if they were served by others.

THE SEARCH FOR LEAVEN

בְּדִיקַת חָמֵץ

On the evening before the Seder (or the evening before that, if the Seder falls on a Sabbath), after dark,
by the light of a lamp or candle, a search is conducted for any leftover pieces of bread or other leavened food
(some is always found, having been deposited in a corner for this express purpose).
On the following morning it is ceremonially burnt or otherwise disposed of.

Before the search, recite:

Blessed are You, our Eternal God, Ruler of the world, who has sanctified us by Your commandments, and enjoined us to remove leavened food from our homes.

בָּרוּךְ אַתָּה יְיָ, אֱלֹהֵינוּ מֶלֶךְ הָעוֹלָם, אֲשֶׁר קִדְּשָׁנוּ בְּמִצְוֹתָיו, וְצִוָּנוּ עַל בִּעוּר חָמֵץ.

After the search, recite:

All hametz in my possession which I have not seen or removed, or of which I am unaware, is hereby nullified and ownerless as the dust of the earth.

כָּל חֲמִירָא וַחֲמִיעָה דְּאִכָּא בִרְשׁוּתִי, דְּלָא חֲמִיתֵּהּ וּדְלָא בְעַרְתֵּהּ וּדְלָא יְדַעְנָא לֵהּ, לִבָּטֵל וְלֶהֱוֵי הֶפְקֵר כְּעַפְרָא דְאַרְעָא.

ORDER FOR THE NIGHT OF PESACH

סֵדֶר לֵיל פֶּסַח

The Sanctification	קַדֵּשׁ
Washing the Hands	וּרְחַץ
Dipping the Karpas	כַּרְפַּס
Breaking the Matzah	יַחַץ
The Narration	מַגִּיד
Washing the Hands	רָחְצָה
Motzi	מוֹצִיא
Matzah	מַצָּה
The Bitter Herbs	מָרוֹר
Herb and Matzah Together	כּוֹרֵךְ
The Meal	שֻׁלְחָן עוֹרֵךְ
Finding the Afikoman	צָפוּן
Thanksgiving for the Meal	בָּרֵךְ
The Hallel after the Meal	הַלֵּל
Concluding Prayer	נִרְצָה

The Hebrew names of the Seder rituals form a rhyme, reminding us of their order. Just as there were fifteen steps leading to the Temple, there are fifteen rituals to perform tonight, leading us to holiness.

KINDLING THE LIGHTS

הַדְלָקַת נֵרוֹת

The lights are kindled.

Blessed are You, our Eternal God, Ruler of the world, who has sanctified us by Your commandments, and enjoined us to kindle the (Sabbath and) Festival lights.

בָּרוּךְ אַתָּה יְיָ אֱלֹהֵינוּ מֶלֶךְ הָעוֹלָם, אֲשֶׁר קִדְּשָׁנוּ בְּמִצְוֹתָיו, וְצִוָּנוּ לְהַדְלִיק נֵר שֶׁל (שַׁבָּת וְשֶׁל) יוֹם טוֹב.

THE SANCTIFICATION AND THE FIRST CUP

קַדֵּשׁ וְכוֹס שֶׁל קִדּוּשׁ

The cups are filled and raised in remembrance of the first promise of redemption, as it is said:

Therefore say to the children of Israel: I am the Eternal One, and I will lead you out from under the Egyptian yoke.

לָכֵן אֱמֹר לִבְנֵי־יִשְׂרָאֵל אֲנִי יְהֹוָה וְהוֹצֵאתִי אֶתְכֶם מִתַּחַת סִבְלֹת מִצְרָיִם.

We drink four cups of wine at the Seder to symbolize God's four promises to the Israelites in the book of Exodus: "I will lead you out from under the Egyptian yoke," "I will deliver you from slavery," "I will redeem you," and "I will take you to be my people." The number four appears again in the Four Questions and the Four Children. What is its significance? Perhaps its symmetry, expressed by the four corners of a square or the four points of a compass, symbolizes completeness and perfection.

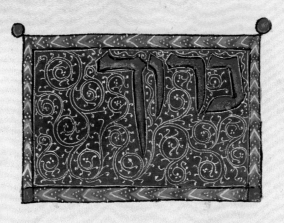

Kiddush for Sabbath Evening

The sixth day: Heaven and earth, and all their array, were finished. For with the seventh day God finished the work of creation, and on the seventh day God rested from all the work, now done. Then God blessed the seventh day and declared it holy, having rested on it from the completed work of creation.

יוֹם הַשִּׁשִּׁי: וַיְכֻלּוּ הַשָּׁמַיִם וְהָאָרֶץ וְכָל־צְבָאָם: וַיְכַל אֱלֹהִים בַּיּוֹם הַשְּׁבִיעִי מְלַאכְתּוֹ אֲשֶׁר עָשָׂה, וַיִּשְׁבֹּת בַּיּוֹם הַשְּׁבִיעִי מִכָּל־מְלַאכְתּוֹ אֲשֶׁר עָשָׂה: וַיְבָרֶךְ אֱלֹהִים אֶת יוֹם הַשְּׁבִיעִי וַיְקַדֵּשׁ אֹתוֹ, כִּי בוֹ שָׁבַת מִכָּל־מְלַאכְתּוֹ, אֲשֶׁר־בָּרָא אֱלֹהִים לַעֲשׂוֹת:

Blessed are You, our Eternal God, Ruler of the world, Creator of the fruit of the vine.

בָּרוּךְ אַתָּה יְיָ אֱלֹהֵינוּ מֶלֶךְ הָעוֹלָם, בּוֹרֵא פְּרִי הַגָּפֶן.

Blessed are You, our Eternal God, Ruler of the world, who has chosen us from all people, and singled us out from among the nations, by sanctifying us through Your commandments. In Your love, Eternal God, You have given us (Sabbaths for rest and) Festivals for gladness, times of celebration and rejoicing. We thank You for this (Sabbath day and for this) Festival of Unleavened Bread, the season of our freedom, when we unite in worship and recall the Exodus from Egypt. For You have chosen us from all peoples to consecrate us to Your service, and (in Your love and kindness) You have entrusted to us (the Sabbath and) the Holy Days for gladness and joy.

בָּרוּךְ אַתָּה יְיָ אֱלֹהֵינוּ מֶלֶךְ הָעוֹלָם, אֲשֶׁר בָּחַר־בָּנוּ מִכָּל־עָם וְרוֹמְמָנוּ מִכָּל־לָשׁוֹן, וְקִדְּשָׁנוּ בְּמִצְוֹתָיו, וַתִּתֶּן־לָנוּ, יְיָ אֱלֹהֵינוּ, בְּאַהֲבָה (שַׁבָּתוֹת לִמְנוּחָה וּ) מוֹעֲדִים לְשִׂמְחָה, חַגִּים וּזְמַנִּים לְשָׂשׂוֹן: אֶת־יוֹם (הַשַּׁבָּת הַזֶּה וְאֶת־יוֹם) חַג הַמַּצּוֹת הַזֶּה, זְמַן חֵרוּתֵנוּ, מִקְרָא קֹדֶשׁ, זֵכֶר לִיצִיאַת מִצְרָיִם. כִּי־בָנוּ בָחַרְתָּ וְאוֹתָנוּ קִדַּשְׁתָּ מִכָּל־הָעַמִּים, (וְשַׁבָּת) וּמוֹעֲדֵי קָדְשֶׁךָ (בְּאַהֲבָה וּבְרָצוֹן,) בְּשִׂמְחָה וּבְשָׂשׂוֹן הִנְחַלְתָּנוּ.

Blessed are You, Eternal One, who sanctifies (the Sabbath,) the House of Israel and the Festivals.

בָּרוּךְ אַתָּה יְיָ, מְקַדֵּשׁ (הַשַּׁבָּת וְ) יִשְׂרָאֵל וְהַזְּמַנִּים.

11

HAVDALAH

הַבְדָּלָה

On Saturday night all look at the Festival lights while the following is said:

Blessed are You, our Eternal God, Ruler of the world, Creator of the flames of fire.

בָּרוּךְ אַתָּה יְיָ, אֱלֹהֵינוּ מֶלֶךְ הָעוֹלָם, בּוֹרֵא מְאוֹרֵי הָאֵשׁ.

Blessed are You, our Eternal God, Ruler of the world, who has taught us to distinguish between holy and common, light and darkness, the House of Israel and the other peoples, the seventh day of rest and the six days of work, the holiness of the Sabbath and that of the Festivals.

בָּרוּךְ אַתָּה יְיָ, אֱלֹהֵינוּ מֶלֶךְ הָעוֹלָם, הַמַּבְדִיל בֵּין קֹדֶשׁ לְחֹל, בֵּין אוֹר לְחֹשֶׁךְ, בֵּין יִשְׂרָאֵל לָעַמִּים, בֵּין יוֹם הַשְּׁבִיעִי לְשֵׁשֶׁת יְמֵי הַמַּעֲשֶׂה. בֵּין קְדֻשַּׁת שַׁבָּת לִקְדֻשַּׁת יוֹם טוֹב הִבְדַּלְתָּ.

Blessed are You, Eternal One, who has taught us to distinguish between holy and holy.

בָּרוּךְ אַתָּה יְיָ, הַמַּבְדִיל בֵּין קֹדֶשׁ לְקֹדֶשׁ.

Blessed are You, our Eternal God, Ruler of the world, who has kept us alive, sustained us and enabled us to reach this season.

בָּרוּךְ אַתָּה יְיָ, אֱלֹהֵינוּ מֶלֶךְ הָעוֹלָם, שֶׁהֶחֱיָנוּ, וְקִיְּמָנוּ, וְהִגִּיעָנוּ לַזְּמַן הַזֶּה.

All lean to the left and drink the First Cup.

WASHING THE HANDS

וּרְחַץ

Wash your hands without reciting the customary blessing.

DIPPING THE KARPAS

טִבּוּל הַכַּרְפַּס

The Karpas is dipped in salt water.

Blessed are You, our Eternal God, Ruler of the world, Creator of the fruit of the earth.

בָּרוּךְ אַתָּה יְיָ, אֱלֹהֵינוּ מֶלֶךְ הָעוֹלָם, בּוֹרֵא פְּרִי הָאֲדָמָה:

The Karpas is eaten.

BREAKING THE MATZAH

יַחַץ

The leader takes out the middle matzah and breaks it in two. The larger piece, known as the Afikoman, will presently be hidden away; the smaller piece is replaced between the two whole matzot, which are raised while the following is recited:

THE NARRATION

מַגִּיד

This is the bread of affliction our ancestors ate in the land of Egypt. Let all who are hungry come and eat; let all who are in need come and share our Passover. This year here, next year in the land of Israel; this year oppressed, next year free.

הָא לַחְמָא עַנְיָא דִי אֲכָלוּ אַבְהָתָנָא בְּאַרְעָא דְמִצְרָיִם. כָּל־דִּכְפִין יֵיתֵי וְיֵכוֹל, כָּל־דִּצְרִיךְ יֵיתֵי וְיִפְסַח. הָשַׁתָּא הָכָא, לְשַׁתָּא דְאָתְיָא בְּאַרְעָא דְיִשְׂרָאֵל; הָשַׁתָּא עַבְדֵי, לְשַׁתָּא דְאָתְיָא בְּנֵי חוֹרִין.

THE FOUR QUESTIONS

אַרְבַּע קֻשִׁיוֹת

It is customary for these questions to be asked by the youngest person who is able to do so.
The Second Cup of wine is filled.

How different is this night from all other nights!

מַה נִּשְׁתַּנָּה הַלַּיְלָה הַזֶּה מִכָּל־הַלֵּילוֹת !

On other nights we eat leavened or unleavened bread: why tonight only unleavened?

שֶׁבְּכָל־הַלֵּילוֹת אָנוּ אוֹכְלִין חָמֵץ וּמַצָּה ; הַלַּיְלָה הַזֶּה כֻּלּוֹ מַצָּה !

On other nights we eat all kinds of herbs: why tonight bitter herbs?

שֶׁבְּכָל־הַלֵּילוֹת אָנוּ אוֹכְלִין שְׁאָר יְרָקוֹת ; הַלַּיְלָה הַזֶּה מָרוֹר !

On other nights we do not dip herbs even once: why tonight twice?

שֶׁבְּכָל־הַלֵּילוֹת אֵין אָנוּ מַטְבִּילִין אֲפִילוּ פַּעַם אֶחָת ; הַלַּיְלָה הַזֶּה שְׁתֵּי פְעָמִים !

On other nights we eat sitting upright or leaning: why do we all lean tonight?

שֶׁבְּכָל־הַלֵּילוֹת אָנוּ אוֹכְלִין בֵּין יוֹשְׁבִין וּבֵין מְסֻבִּין ; הַלַּיְלָה הַזֶּה כֻּלָּנוּ מְסֻבִּין !

Questioning is a sign of freedom—the freedom to explore and discover. In asking questions, each person finds his or her own meaning in the Passover Seder.

Here, the figure pouring wine reminds us of the Mishnaic requirement that the Second Cup of wine should be filled as we ask the Four Questions.

Our story begins with degradation; our telling ends with glory.

We were slaves to Pharaoh in Egypt and our Eternal God led us out from there with a mighty hand and an outstretched arm. If the Holy One, ever to be blessed, had not led our ancestors out of Egypt, we and our children and children's children would have remained slaves to Pharaoh in Egypt. Therefore even if we were all wise and discerning, all scholars and experts in Torah, it would still be our duty to retell the story of the Exodus: and those who linger over the telling are worthy of praise.

No free person can know what it is like to be a slave. We must keep alive the memory so that we never take our freedom for granted or let others be enslaved.

מַתְחִיל בִּגְנוּת, וּמְסַיֵּם בְּשֶׁבַח.

עֲבָדִים הָיִינוּ לְפַרְעֹה בְּמִצְרַיִם, וַיּוֹצִיאֵנוּ יְיָ אֱלֹהֵינוּ מִשָּׁם בְּיָד חֲזָקָה וּבִזְרוֹעַ נְטוּיָה. וְאִלּוּ לֹא הוֹצִיא הַקָּדוֹשׁ בָּרוּךְ הוּא אֶת־אֲבוֹתֵינוּ מִמִּצְרַיִם, הֲרֵי אָנוּ וּבָנֵינוּ וּבְנֵי בָנֵינוּ מְשֻׁעְבָּדִים הָיִינוּ לְפַרְעֹה בְּמִצְרָיִם. וַאֲפִילוּ כֻּלָּנוּ חֲכָמִים, כֻּלָּנוּ נְבוֹנִים, כֻּלָּנוּ זְקֵנִים, כֻּלָּנוּ יוֹדְעִים אֶת־הַתּוֹרָה, מִצְוָה עָלֵינוּ לְסַפֵּר בִּיצִיאַת מִצְרָיִם, וְכָל־הַמַּרְבֶּה לְסַפֵּר בִּיצִיאַת מִצְרַיִם הֲרֵי זֶה מְשֻׁבָּח.

There is a story about Rabbi Eliezer, Rabbi Joshua, Rabbi El'azar ben Azariah, Rabbi Akiva, and Rabbi Tarfon, who were sitting in B'nei B'rak. All that night they talked about the Exodus, until their students came and told them: "Rabbis, it is time to recite the morning Shema!"

Rabbi El'azar ben Azariah said: "I seem like a man of seventy, yet I never understood why we must tell of the Exodus at night until Ben Zoma came along with this teaching: 'Remember the day you went out of Egypt all the days of your life' (Deut. 16.3), meaning that we must remember our liberation during the night, too."

The Sages saw an additional lesson in this verse: "The days of your life" are your days in this world—the world as it is; "All the days of your life" includes the messianic days.

מַעֲשֶׂה בְּרַבִּי אֱלִיעֶזֶר וְרַבִּי יְהוֹשֻׁעַ וְרַבִּי אֶלְעָזָר בֶּן־עֲזַרְיָה וְרַבִּי עֲקִיבָא, וְרַבִּי טַרְפוֹן שֶׁהָיוּ מְסֻבִּין בִּבְנֵי־בְרַק, וְהָיוּ מְסַפְּרִים בִּיצִיאַת מִצְרַיִם כָּל־אוֹתוֹ הַלַּיְלָה, עַד שֶׁבָּאוּ תַלְמִידֵיהֶם וְאָמְרוּ לָהֶם: "רַבּוֹתֵינוּ, הִגִּיעַ זְמַן קְרִיאַת־שְׁמַע שֶׁל שַׁחֲרִית!"

אָמַר רַבִּי אֶלְעָזָר בֶּן־עֲזַרְיָה: הֲרֵי אֲנִי כְּבֶן שִׁבְעִים שָׁנָה. וְלֹא זָכִיתִי שֶׁתֵּאָמֵר יְצִיאַת מִצְרַיִם בַּלֵּילוֹת, עַד שֶׁדְּרָשָׁהּ בֶּן זוֹמָא. שֶׁנֶּאֱמַר: לְמַעַן תִּזְכֹּר אֶת־יוֹם צֵאתְךָ מֵאֶרֶץ מִצְרַיִם כֹּל יְמֵי חַיֶּיךָ. יְמֵי חַיֶּיךָ: הַיָּמִים. כֹּל יְמֵי חַיֶּיךָ: הַלֵּילוֹת.

וַחֲכָמִים אוֹמְרִים: יְמֵי חַיֶּיךָ: הָעוֹלָם הַזֶּה. כֹּל יְמֵי חַיֶּיךָ: לְהָבִיא לִימוֹת הַמָּשִׁיחַ.

There has been much speculation about why the rabbis' students had to tell them that it was time for morning prayers. Why were their students not with them? Why did the rabbis spend the entire night discussing the Exodus? During the Bar Kochba revolt when the Jews sought to overthrow the Romans (132–135 C.E.), these rabbis were forbidden to teach Torah. Perhaps this episode took place when they were hiding from their enemy in underground tunnels, and they could not see the sunrise. Perhaps it was too dangerous for their students to study with them. Perhaps they were retelling the story of the Exodus all night in the hope that one day soon they, too, would be free. We will never know the answers to these questions, but the five rabbis remind us that Jews have retold the story of the Exodus in many places of persecution and suffering, and it is the story of freedom itself that keeps hope alive.

Praised be the Eternal who is everywhere.
Praised be the Eternal.
Praised be the One who gave the Torah to the people of Israel.
Praised be the Eternal.

בָּרוּךְ הַמָּקוֹם.

בָּרוּךְ הוּא.

בָּרוּךְ שֶׁנָּתַן תּוֹרָה לְעַמּוֹ יִשְׂרָאֵל.

בָּרוּךְ הוּא.

THE FOUR CHILDREN

אַרְבָּעָה בָנִים

Because children are different from one another, they each learn a different lesson about the Passover story.

The Torah alludes to four types of child: one who is wise, one who is wicked, one who is simple, and one who does not know how to ask.

What does the wise one say? "What are the duties, laws, and precepts which our Eternal God has commanded us?" To this child teach all the laws of Pesach, even the difficult law that one concludes the Pesach meal with the Afikoman.

What does the wicked one say? "What is this service to you?" To *you*, but not to me! If some should cut themselves off from the community and scorn our faith, make them eat their words, telling them: "I do this because of what God did for me when I came out of Egypt." For *me*, but not for you! For, had you been there, you would not have been redeemed.

What does the simple one say? "What is this?" And you shall answer: "With a mighty hand God led us out of Egypt, out of the house of bondage."

כְּנֶגֶד אַרְבָּעָה בָנִים דִּבְּרָה תוֹרָה: אֶחָד חָכָם, וְאֶחָד רָשָׁע, וְאֶחָד תָּם, וְאֶחָד שֶׁאֵינוֹ יוֹדֵעַ לִשְׁאוֹל.

חָכָם מַה הוּא אוֹמֵר? "מָה הָעֵדֹת וְהַחֻקִּים וְהַמִּשְׁפָּטִים אֲשֶׁר צִוָּה יְיָ אֱלֹהֵינוּ אֹתָנוּ?" וְאַף אַתָּה אֱמָר־לוֹ כְּהִלְכוֹת הַפֶּסַח, "אֵין מַפְטִירִין אַחַר הַפֶּסַח אֲפִיקוֹמָן."

רָשָׁע מַה הוּא אוֹמֵר? "מָה הָעֲבוֹדָה הַזֹּאת לָכֶם?" לָכֶם וְלֹא לוֹ! וּלְפִי שֶׁהוֹצִיא אֶת־עַצְמוֹ מִן הַכְּלָל, וְכָפַר בָּעִקָּר, אַף אַתָּה הַקְהֵה אֶת־שִׁנָּיו וֶאֱמָר־לוֹ: "בַּעֲבוּר זֶה עָשָׂה יְיָ לִי בְּצֵאתִי מִמִּצְרָיִם." לִי וְלֹא־לוֹ! אִלּוּ הָיָה שָׁם, לֹא הָיָה נִגְאָל.

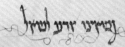

תָּם מַה הוּא אוֹמֵר? "מַה זֹּאת?" וְאָמַרְתָּ אֵלָיו: "בְּחֹזֶק יָד הוֹצִיאָנוּ יְיָ מִמִּצְרַיִם, מִבֵּית עֲבָדִים."

And with the one who does not know how to ask, *you* must take the first step, as it is said: "You shall tell your child on that day…"

וְשֶׁאֵינוֹ יוֹדֵעַ לִשְׁאוֹל, אַתְּ פְּתַח לוֹ, שֶׁנֶּאֱמַר: "וְהִגַּדְתָּ לְבִנְךָ בַּיּוֹם הַהוּא…".

Perhaps there is a wise child within each of us, just as there is a wicked child, a simple child, and one who does not know how to ask. All these characteristics are part of our Jewish lives and are reflected in the way we approach the Seder.

IN THE BEGINNING

מִתְּחִלָּה

In the beginning our ancestors were idol worshippers, but now we have learned to worship the true God, as it is said: "Then Joshua spoke to all the people, 'Thus says the Eternal God of Israel: Long ago in the days of Terach, the father of Abraham and Nachor, your ancestors lived beyond the River, and worshipped other gods. Then I took your forefather Abraham from beyond the River, and led him all over the land of Canaan. I blessed him with many descendants, for I gave him Isaac, and to Isaac I gave Jacob and Esau; and I let Esau take possession of Mount Seir. But Jacob and his children went down to Egypt.'"

מִתְּחִלָּה עוֹבְדֵי עֲבוֹדָה זָרָה הָיוּ אֲבוֹתֵינוּ, וְעַכְשָׁו קֵרְבָנוּ הַמָּקוֹם לַעֲבוֹדָתוֹ, שֶׁנֶּאֱמַר: "וַיֹּאמֶר יְהוֹשֻׁעַ אֶל־כָּל־הָעָם, כֹּה־אָמַר יְיָ אֱלֹהֵי יִשְׂרָאֵל, בְּעֵבֶר הַנָּהָר יָשְׁבוּ אֲבוֹתֵיכֶם מֵעוֹלָם, תֶּרַח אֲבִי אַבְרָהָם וַאֲבִי נָחוֹר, וַיַּעַבְדוּ אֱלֹהִים אֲחֵרִים. וָאֶקַּח אֶת־ אֲבִיכֶם אֶת־אַבְרָהָם מֵעֵבֶר הַנָּהָר, וָאוֹלֵךְ אוֹתוֹ בְּכָל־אֶרֶץ כְּנַעַן, וָאַרְבֶּה אֶת־זַרְעוֹ, וָאֶתֶּן־לוֹ אֶת־יִצְחָק, וָאֶתֵּן לְיִצְחָק אֶת־ יַעֲקֹב וְאֶת־עֵשָׂו, וָאֶתֵּן לְעֵשָׂו אֶת־הַר שֵׂעִיר לָרֶשֶׁת אוֹתוֹ, וְיַעֲקֹב וּבָנָיו יָרְדוּ מִצְרָיִם:"

Abraham was the first person to recognize that there is only one God and promised to obey God's commands. In return, God promised to protect the Israelites. It was this covenant between God and Abraham that began the special relationship Jews have with God. Based on moral responsibility, it includes living by values that are essential to freedom: justice and compassion.

Blessed be the One who keeps the divine promise to Israel, blessed be the One.

בָּרוּךְ שׁוֹמֵר הַבְטָחָתוֹ לְיִשְׂרָאֵל, בָּרוּךְ הוּא.

The covenant between God and the Jewish people is so important that at this moment in the Seder, we lift our wineglasses as if to toast this promise, but we do not drink.

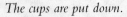

The cups are raised.

That promise has sustained our ancestors, and it sustains us still. For not one enemy alone has sought to destroy us, but in every generation enemies seek to destroy us, but the Holy One, ever to be blessed, delivers us from their power.

וְהִיא שֶׁעָמְדָה לַאֲבוֹתֵינוּ וְלָנוּ, שֶׁלֹּא אֶחָד בִּלְבָד עָמַד עָלֵינוּ לְכַלוֹתֵנוּ, אֶלָּא שֶׁבְּכָל־דּוֹר וָדוֹר עוֹמְדִים עָלֵינוּ לְכַלוֹתֵנוּ, וְהַקָּדוֹשׁ בָּרוּךְ הוּא מַצִּילֵנוּ מִיָּדָם.

The cups are put down.

A WANDERING ARAMEAN

אֲרַמִּי אֹבֵד אָבִי

A wandering Aramean was my father: and he went down to Egypt, and lived there as a stranger, with only a few people. There he became a great nation, powerful and numerous. But the Egyptians ill-treated us: they afflicted us, and imposed hard labor upon us. Then we cried to the Eternal One, God of our ancestors; and God heard our cry; and saw our affliction, our misery, our oppression. Then God brought us out of Egypt with a mighty hand and an outstretched arm, with awesome power, with signs and wonders.

אֲרַמִּי אֹבֵד אָבִי, וַיֵּרֶד מִצְרַיְמָה וַיָּגָר שָׁם בִּמְתֵי מְעָט, וַיְהִי שָׁם לְגוֹי גָּדוֹל, עָצוּם וָרָב. וַיָּרֵעוּ אֹתָנוּ הַמִּצְרִים וַיְעַנּוּנוּ. וַיִּתְּנוּ עָלֵינוּ עֲבֹדָה קָשָׁה. וַנִּצְעַק אֶל־יְיָ אֱלֹהֵי אֲבֹתֵינוּ, וַיִּשְׁמַע יְיָ אֶת־קֹלֵנוּ, וַיַּרְא אֶת־עָנְיֵנוּ וְאֶת־עֲמָלֵנוּ וְאֶת לַחֲצֵנוּ. וַיּוֹצִאֵנוּ יְיָ מִמִּצְרַיִם בְּיָד חֲזָקָה וּבִזְרֹעַ נְטוּיָה, וּבְמֹרָא גָּדוֹל וּבְאֹתוֹת וּבְמוֹפְתִים.

A Wandering Aramean Was My Father: and He Went Down to Egypt

He was impelled by a force of the divine word, as it is written: "Know for a certainty that your offspring shall be strangers in a strange land and they shall be enslaved and afflicted for four hundred years." (Gen. 15.13)

And Lived There as a Stranger, with Only a Few People

"And lived there" indicates that your ancestor Jacob never planned to sink roots there, but only to stay for a while, as it is said: "And Joseph's brothers said to Pharaoh, 'Only to sojourn in the land have we come, for there is no food for our flocks in the land of Canaan.'" (Gen. 47.4)

Your ancestors numbered seventy souls when they went down to Egypt, and now your Eternal God has made you as numerous as the stars of heaven. (Deut. 10.22)

It was not because you were more in number than any other people that the love of the Eternal One was set upon you and you were chosen, for you were the fewest of all peoples; but because God loves you, and is keeping the solemn promise which was made to your ancestors. (Deut. 7.7-8)

אֲרַמִּי אֹבֵד אָבִי וַיֵּרֶד מִצְרַיְמָה

אֲרַמִּי אֹבֵד אָבִי וַיֵּרֶד מִצְרַיְמָה. אָנוּס עַל פִּי הַדִּבּוּר, כְּמָה שֶׁנֶּאֱמַר: יָדֹעַ תֵּדַע כִּי־גֵר יִהְיֶה זַרְעֲךָ בְּאֶרֶץ לֹא לָהֶם, וַעֲבָדוּם וְעִנּוּ אֹתָם אַרְבַּע מֵאוֹת שָׁנָה.

וַיָּגָר שָׁם בִּמְתֵי מְעָט

וַיָּגָר שָׁם. מְלַמֵּד שֶׁלֹּא יָרַד יַעֲקֹב לְהִשְׁתַּקֵּעַ בְּמִצְרַיִם אֶלָּא לָגוּר שָׁם. שֶׁנֶּאֱמַר: וַיֹּאמְרוּ אֶל־פַּרְעֹה לָגוּר בָּאָרֶץ בָּאנוּ כִּי־אֵין מִרְעֶה לַצֹּאן אֲשֶׁר לַעֲבָדֶיךָ כִּי־כָבֵד הָרָעָב בְּאֶרֶץ כְּנָעַן. וְעַתָּה יֵשְׁבוּ־נָא עֲבָדֶיךָ בְּאֶרֶץ גֹּשֶׁן:

בְּשִׁבְעִים נֶפֶשׁ יָרְדוּ אֲבֹתֶיךָ מִצְרַיְמָה, וְעַתָּה, שָׂמְךָ יְיָ אֱלֹהֶיךָ, כְּכוֹכְבֵי הַשָּׁמַיִם לָרֹב.

לֹא מֵרֻבְּכֶם מִכָּל־הָעַמִּים חָשַׁק יְיָ בָּכֶם וַיִּבְחַר בָּכֶם, כִּי־אַתֶּם הַמְעַט מִכָּל־הָעַמִּים, כִּי מֵאַהֲבַת יְיָ אֶתְכֶם וּמִשָּׁמְרוֹ אֶת־הַשְּׁבֻעָה אֲשֶׁר נִשְׁבַּע לַאֲבֹתֵיכֶם.

There He Became a Great Nation

The fact that it says "nation" shows that the Israelites remained distinctive.

On the strength of four virtues were the Israelites redeemed from Egypt: they did not change their names; they did not change their language; they did not speak evil; and they did not give up their moral standards. (Melchita to Ex. 12.6)

Powerful and Numerous

The Israelites were fruitful and prolific; they increased in number and became very powerful, until the land was full of them. (Ex. 1.7)

But the Egyptians Ill-Treated Us

Now a new king arose over Egypt, who did not know Joseph, and he said to his people: "This people Israel is too numerous and powerful for us. Come, let us deal shrewdly with them, lest they increase further and, in the event of war, join our enemies and fight against us, and then escape from our land." (Ex. 1.8-10)

וַיְהִי שָׁם לְגוֹי גָּדוֹל

"וַיְהִי שָׁם לְגוֹי" מְלַמֵּד שֶׁהָיוּ יִשְׂרָאֵל מְצֻיָּנִים שָׁם.
בִּזְכוּת אַרְבָּעָה דְּבָרִים נִגְאֲלוּ יִשְׂרָאֵל מִמִּצְרָיִם: שֶׁלֹּא שִׁנּוּ אֶת־שְׁמָם; וְלֹא שִׁנּוּ אֶת־לְשׁוֹנָם; וְלֹא אָמְרוּ לְשׁוֹן הָרָע; וְלֹא נִמְצָא בָּהֶן אֶחָד פָּרוּץ בְּעֶרְוָה.

עָצוּם וָרָב

וּבְנֵי יִשְׂרָאֵל פָּרוּ וַיִּשְׁרְצוּ, וַיִּרְבּוּ וַיַּעַצְמוּ בִּמְאֹד מְאֹד, וַתִּמָּלֵא הָאָרֶץ אֹתָם.

וַיָּרֵעוּ אֹתָנוּ הַמִּצְרִים

וַיָּקָם מֶלֶךְ־חָדָשׁ עַל־מִצְרָיִם, אֲשֶׁר לֹא־יָדַע אֶת־יוֹסֵף, וַיֹּאמֶר אֶל־עַמּוֹ: "הִנֵּה עַם בְּנֵי יִשְׂרָאֵל רַב וְעָצוּם מִמֶּנּוּ. הָבָה נִתְחַכְּמָה לוֹ, פֶּן־יִרְבֶּה וְהָיָה כִּי־תִקְרֶאנָה מִלְחָמָה וְנוֹסַף גַּם־הוּא עַל־שֹׂנְאֵינוּ, וְנִלְחַם־בָּנוּ, וְעָלָה מִן־הָאָרֶץ."

THEY AFFLICTED US

They set taskmasters over them, to afflict them with forced labor; thus they built for Pharaoh store-cities, such as Pithom and Raamses. (Ex. 1.11)

AND IMPOSED HARD LABOR UPON US

The Egyptians subjected the Israelites to cruel slavery, and made their life bitter through hard labor with clay and bricks, and all kinds of work in the fields. (Ex. 1.13-14)

THEN WE CRIED TO THE ETERNAL ONE, GOD OF OUR ANCESTORS

After many long years, the king of Egypt died. But the children of Israel still groaned under their bondage, and cried out; and the cry wrung from them by their bondage ascended to God. (Ex. 2.23)

וַיְעַנּוּנוּ

וַיָּשִׂימוּ עָלָיו שָׂרֵי מִסִּים, לְמַעַן עַנֹּתוֹ בְּסִבְלֹתָם, וַיִּבֶן עָרֵי מִסְכְּנוֹת לְפַרְעֹה, אֶת־פִּתֹם וְאֶת־רַעַמְסֵס.

וַיִּתְּנוּ עָלֵינוּ עֲבֹדָה קָשָׁה

וַיַּעֲבִדוּ מִצְרַיִם אֶת־בְּנֵי יִשְׂרָאֵל בְּפָרֶךְ, וַיְמָרְרוּ אֶת־חַיֵּיהֶם בַּעֲבֹדָה קָשָׁה בְּחֹמֶר וּבִלְבֵנִים, וּבְכָל־עֲבֹדָה בַּשָּׂדֶה.

וַנִּצְעַק אֶל־יְיָ אֱלֹהֵי אֲבֹתֵינוּ

וַיְהִי בַיָּמִים הָרַבִּים הָהֵם וַיָּמָת מֶלֶךְ מִצְרַיִם, וַיֵּאָנְחוּ בְנֵי־יִשְׂרָאֵל מִן־הָעֲבֹדָה וַיִּזְעָקוּ, וַתַּעַל שַׁוְעָתָם אֶל־הָאֱלֹהִים מִן־הָעֲבֹדָה.

AND GOD HEARD OUR CRY

God heard their groans, and God remembered the covenant with Abraham, with Isaac, and with Jacob. (Ex. 2.24)

AND SAW OUR AFFLICTION

And God said: "I have indeed seen the affliction of my people in Egypt, and heard their cry against their taskmasters; for I know their pains." (Ex. 3.7)

This refers particularly to the breaking up of their family life, as it is said: "God saw the children of Israel, and God knew." (Ex. 2.25)

OUR MISERY

This refers particularly to the murder of their children, as it is said: "Every firstborn that is born to the Hebrews you shall throw into the Nile." (Ex. 1.22)

God was grieved at the misery of Israel. (Judges 10.16)

In all their afflictions, God was afflicted. (Isa. 63.9)

Wherever they went into exile, the Divine Presence went with them. When they were exiled to Egypt, the Divine Presence went with them; in Babylon, the Divine Presence was with them; and until their final redemption, God will remain in exile with them. (Babylonian Talmud Megillah 29a)

OUR OPPRESSION

Now the cry of the children of Israel has reached me, and I have seen the oppression which the Egyptians are inflicting upon them. (Ex. 3.9)

וַיִּשְׁמַע יְיָ אֶת־קֹלֵנוּ

וַיִּשְׁמַע אֱלֹהִים אֶת־נַאֲקָתָם, וַיִּזְכֹּר אֱלֹהִים אֶת־בְּרִיתוֹ אֶת־אַבְרָהָם, אֶת־יִצְחָק וְאֶת־יַעֲקֹב.

וַיַּרְא אֶת־עָנְיֵנוּ

וַיֹּאמֶר יְיָ: רָאֹה רָאִיתִי אֶת־עֳנִי עַמִּי אֲשֶׁר בְּמִצְרָיִם, וְאֶת־צַעֲקָתָם שָׁמַעְתִּי מִפְּנֵי נֹגְשָׂיו, כִּי יָדַעְתִּי אֶת־מַכְאֹבָיו.

זוֹ פְּרִישׁוּת דֶּרֶךְ אֶרֶץ, כְּמוֹ שֶׁנֶּאֱמַר: וַיַּרְא אֱלֹהִים אֶת־בְּנֵי יִשְׂרָאֵל, וַיֵּדַע אֱלֹהִים.

וְאֶת־עֲמָלֵנוּ

אֵלוּ הַבָּנִים, כְּמוֹ שֶׁנֶּאֱמַר: כָּל־הַבֵּן הַיִּלּוֹד הַיְאֹרָה תַּשְׁלִיכֻהוּ.

וַתִּקְצַר נַפְשׁוֹ בַּעֲמַל יִשְׂרָאֵל.

בְּכָל־צָרָתָם לוֹ צָר.

בְּכָל־מָקוֹם שֶׁגָּלוּ, שְׁכִינָה עִמָּהֶן. גָּלוּ לְמִצְרַיִם, שְׁכִינָה עִמָּהֶן; גָּלוּ לְבָבֶל, שְׁכִינָה עִמָּהֶן; וְאַף כְּשֶׁהֵן עֲתִידִין לִגָּאֵל, שְׁכִינָה עִמָּהֶן.

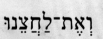

וְאֶת־לַחֲצֵנוּ

וְעַתָּה הִנֵּה צַעֲקַת בְּנֵי־יִשְׂרָאֵל בָּאָה אֵלָי, וְגַם־רָאִיתִי אֶת־הַלַּחַץ אֲשֶׁר מִצְרַיִם לֹחֲצִים אֹתָם.

THEN GOD BROUGHT US OUT OF EGYPT

Not by an angel, not by a seraph, not by an intermediary; but the Holy One, ever to be blessed, in solitary glory. (Palestinian Talmud)

WITH A MIGHTY HAND AND AN OUTSTRETCHED ARM, WITH AWESOME POWER, WITH SIGNS AND WONDERS

This refers to the revelation of the Divine Presence, as it is said: "Did ever a 'god' attempt to come and take a nation for itself from the midst of another nation by trials, signs, and wonders, and by war, with a mighty hand and an outstretched arm, and with awesome power, all of which your Eternal God did for you in Egypt before your very eyes?" (Deut. 4.34)

וַיּוֹצִאֵנוּ יְיָ מִמִּצְרַיִם
לֹא עַל־יְדֵי מַלְאָךְ, וְלֹא עַל־יְדֵי
שָׂרָף, וְלֹא עַל־יְדֵי שָׁלִיחַ, אֶלָּא
הַקָּדוֹשׁ בָּרוּךְ הוּא בִּכְבוֹדוֹ וּבְעַצְמוֹ.

בְּיָד חֲזָקָה וּבִזְרוֹעַ נְטוּיָה
וּבְמוֹרָא גָּדוֹל וּבְאֹתוֹת
וּבְמוֹפְתִים
זֶה גִּלּוּי שְׁכִינָה, כְּמוֹ שֶׁנֶּאֱמַר: "אוֹ
הֲנִסָּה אֱלֹהִים לָבוֹא לָקַחַת לוֹ גוֹי
מִקֶּרֶב גּוֹי בְּמַסֹּת בְּאֹתֹת וּבְמוֹפְתִים
וּבְמִלְחָמָה וּבְיָד חֲזָקָה וּבִזְרוֹעַ
נְטוּיָה וּבְמוֹרָאִים גְּדֹלִים כְּכֹל אֲשֶׁר־
עָשָׂה לָכֶם יְיָ אֱלֹהֵיכֶם בְּמִצְרַיִם
לְעֵינֶיךָ ?"

This passage and its rabbinic interpretations refer to Jacob as a wandering Aramean who settles in Egypt. Ever since, Jews have been known as a wandering people, settling in countries all over the world. Because of this, we have been influenced by different customs and traditions, as these illuminations illustrate. For example, some illuminated haggadot feature the motif of hare hunting. This comes from the Hebrew mnemonic that reminds us of the order of the beginning of the Seder on the Sabbath— YaKeNHAZ, comprising blessings over the wine (*yayin*); the sanctification (*kiddush*) of the festival; the candle (*ner*) lit when the Sabbath ends; the separation (*havdalah*) of the Sabbath from weekdays; and the thanksgiving blessing for having reached this festive time (*zeman*). To Ashkenazi Jews, YaKeNHAZ sounded like the German *jagen-has,* "hare hunt." Perhaps it was out of empathy with the plight of the hare that it became a well-used image in haggadot. Christian illuminations from Psalters and Books of Hours, popular in medieval Europe, also influenced Hebrew illuminations, particularly in their use of color.

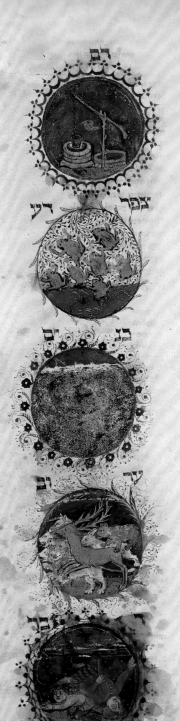

THE TEN PLAGUES

עֶשֶׂר מַכּוֹת

These are the Ten Plagues which the Holy One brought upon the Egyptians:

אֵלּוּ עֶשֶׂר מַכּוֹת שֶׁהֵבִיא הַקָּדוֹשׁ בָּרוּךְ הוּא עַל-הַמִּצְרִים:

It is customary, at the mention of each plague, to spill one drop of wine.

Blood	דָּם
Frogs	צְפַרְדֵּעַ
Lice	כִּנִּים
Wild Beasts	עָרוֹב
Cattle Disease	דֶּבֶר
Boils	שְׁחִין
Hail	בָּרָד
Locusts	אַרְבֶּה
Darkness	חוֹשֶׁךְ
Death of the Firstborn	מַכַּת בְּכוֹרוֹת

Although the plagues successfully forced the Egyptians to let the Israelites go, we do not rejoice in the suffering caused to our taskmasters. On the contrary, we diminish the joy of our celebration by spilling a drop of wine from our cups as we recite each plague. This acknowledgment of the pain inflicted upon the Egyptians reminds us that our freedom should never be at the expense of any other. The drops of wine also symbolize God's tears, shed when the Egyptians drowned, as recorded in the Midrash.

These zodiac-like medallions encapsulating the pictures suggest a play on the round shape of matzah. However, this design may have been influenced by artists of the period who tended to place related subjects in groups of medallions. Opposite, the artist displays his mastery of French Gothic style in the hairstyles and poses of the figures.

It Would Have Been Enough (Dayenu)

דַּיֵּנוּ

How many acts of kindness God has performed for us!
Had God brought us out of Egypt without carrying out judgments against the Egyptians—
Dayenu!

Had God carried out judgments against the Egyptians without vanquishing their Gods—
Dayenu!

Had God vanquished their gods without dividing the sea for us—
Dayenu!

Had God divided the sea for us without leading us across on dry land—
Dayenu!

Had God led us across on dry land without taking care of us for forty years in the desert—
Dayenu!

Had God taken care of us for forty years in the desert without feeding us manna—
Dayenu!

Had God fed us manna without giving us Shabbat—
Dayenu!

כַּמָּה מַעֲלוֹת טוֹבוֹת לַמָּקוֹם עָלֵינוּ:
אִלּוּ הוֹצִיאָנוּ מִמִּצְרַיִם
וְלֹא עָשָׂה בָהֶם שְׁפָטִים-
דַּיֵּנוּ !

אִלּוּ עָשָׂה בָהֶם שְׁפָטִים
וְלֹא עָשָׂה בֵאלֹהֵיהֶם-
דַּיֵּנוּ !

אִלּוּ עָשָׂה בֵאלֹהֵיהֶם
וְלֹא קָרַע לָנוּ אֶת-הַיָּם-
דַּיֵּנוּ !

אִלּוּ קָרַע לָנוּ אֶת-הַיָּם
וְלֹא הֶעֱבִירָנוּ בְתוֹכוֹ בֶּחָרָבָה-
דַּיֵּנוּ !

אִלּוּ הֶעֱבִירָנוּ בְתוֹכוֹ בֶּחָרָבָה
וְלֹא סִפֵּק צָרְכֵּנוּ בַּמִּדְבָּר אַרְבָּעִים שָׁנָה.
דַּיֵּנוּ !

אִלּוּ סִפֵּק צָרְכֵּנוּ בַּמִּדְבָּר אַרְבָּעִים שָׁנָה
וְלֹא הֶאֱכִילָנוּ אֶת-הַמָּן-
דַּיֵּנוּ !

אִלּוּ הֶאֱכִילָנוּ אֶת-הַמָּן
וְלֹא נָתַן לָנוּ אֶת-הַשַּׁבָּת-
דַּיֵּנוּ !

Had God given us Shabbat without bringing us to Mount Sinai—
Dayenu!

Had God brought us to Mount Sinai without giving us the Torah—
Dayenu!

Had God given us the Torah without leading us to the land of Israel—
Dayenu!

Had God led us to the land of Israel without building the Temple for us—
Dayenu!

How manifold and miraculous are the great deeds that our God has performed for us, from taking us out of Egypt to building the Temple.

אִלּוּ נָתַן לָנוּ אֶת־הַשַּׁבָּת
וְלֹא קֵרְבָנוּ לִפְנֵי הַר סִינַי-
דַּיֵּנוּ !

אִלּוּ קֵרְבָנוּ לִפְנֵי הַר סִינַי
וְלֹא נָתַן לָנוּ אֶת־הַתּוֹרָה-
דַּיֵּנוּ !

אִלּוּ נָתַן לָנוּ אֶת־הַתּוֹרָה
וְלֹא הִכְנִיסָנוּ לְאֶרֶץ יִשְׂרָאֵל-
דַּיֵּנוּ !

אִלּוּ הִכְנִיסָנוּ לְאֶרֶץ יִשְׂרָאֵל
וְלֹא בָנָה לָנוּ אֶת־בֵּית
הַבְּחִירָה-
דַּיֵּנוּ !

עַל אַחַת כַּמָּה וְכַמָּה טוֹבָה
כְפוּלָה וּמְכֻפֶּלֶת לַמָּקוֹם עָלֵינוּ
שֶׁכֵּן עָשָׂה כָּל הַנִּפְלָאוֹת הָאֵלֶּה
מִיצִיאַת מִצְרַיִם עַד בִּנְיַן בֵּית
הַבְּחִירָה.

The verses of this song list the many times that we have had reason to be grateful to God, and express how God did more for us than we ever expected. Today, there is a custom of adding contemporary and personal "dayenus" to the song: Had God provided for us in the lands of our dispersion without giving us a homeland, it would have been enough! Had God given us a homeland without enabling us to make the desert bloom, it would have been enough! This acknowledges that in our own lives, we hope to move toward better times, step by step, counting our blessings along the way.

The inscriptions on these ornate, vertical panels repeat the word "illu" (had God) on the right and "ve-lo" (without) on the left, emphasizing the connection between the key words of the Dayenu. Some scholars regard the use of repeated words as the most traditional decorative device in illuminated haggadot.

COURSES OF THE MEAL

Rabban Gamaliel used to say: "If, on Passover, you do not explain these three things, you have not fulfilled your obligation: Pesach, Matzah, and Maror."

הַסְּעוּדָה

רַבָּן גַּמְלִיאֵל הָיָה אוֹמֵר: כָּל־שֶׁלֹּא אָמַר שְׁלֹשָׁה דְּבָרִים אֵלּוּ בַּפֶּסַח, לֹא יָצָא יְדֵי חוֹבָתוֹ. וְאֵלּוּ הֵן: פֶּסַח, מַצָּה וּמָרוֹר.

Rabban Gamaliel makes a simple but important statement about the special foods of the Seder: We do not eat them merely for their own sake, but they are there to help re-create the experience of the Exodus. As Jews, we often identify ourselves by the food we eat—these special foods give us a taste for freedom.

The leader holds up the lamb bone.

PESACH

פֶּסַח

Why, in the days when the Temple still stood, did our ancestors eat at this time a "Passover" lamb? Because the Holy One, ever to be blessed, passed over the houses of our ancestors in Egypt, as it is said: "It is a Passover offering to God, who passed over the houses of the Israelites in Egypt, striking the Egyptians but sparing our houses." (Ex.12.27)

פֶּסַח שֶׁהָיוּ אֲבוֹתֵינוּ
אוֹכְלִים בִּזְמַן שֶׁבֵּית־
הַמִּקְדָּשׁ קַיָּם, עַל שׁוּם
מָה? עַל שׁוּם שֶׁפָּסַח
הַקָּדוֹשׁ בָּרוּךְ הוּא עַל בָּתֵּי
אֲבוֹתֵינוּ בְּמִצְרַיִם, שֶׁנֶּאֱמַר,
"וַאֲמַרְתֶּם: זֶבַח־פֶּסַח הוּא
לַיְיָ, אֲשֶׁר פָּסַח עַל־בָּתֵּי
בְנֵי־יִשְׂרָאֵל בְּמִצְרַיִם,
בְּנָגְפּוֹ אֶת־מִצְרַיִם, וְאֶת־
בָּתֵּינוּ הִצִּיל."

The leader holds up the matzah plate.

MATZAH

Why do we eat this unleavened bread? Because our ancestors did not have time to let their dough ferment before the true Ruler, the Holy One, ever to be blessed, was revealed to them and redeemed them, as we read: "They baked the dough they had brought out of Egypt into cakes of unleavened bread, for they were driven out of Egypt so that they could not delay to prepare food for themselves." (Ex.12.39)

מַצָּה

מַצָּה זוֹ שֶׁאָנוּ אוֹכְלִים עַל שׁוּם מָה? עַל שׁוּם שֶׁלֹא הִסְפִּיק בְּצֵקָם שֶׁל אֲבוֹתֵינוּ לְהַחֲמִיץ עַד שֶׁנִּגְלָה עֲלֵיהֶם מֶלֶךְ מַלְכֵי הַמְּלָכִים, הַקָּדוֹשׁ בָּרוּךְ הוּא וּגְאָלָם. שֶׁנֶּאֱמַר: "וַיֹּאפוּ אֶת־הַבָּצֵק אֲשֶׁר הוֹצִיאוּ מִמִּצְרַיִם עֻגֹת מַצּוֹת, כִּי לֹא חָמֵץ, כִּי־גֹרְשׁוּ מִמִּצְרַיִם וְלֹא יָכְלוּ לְהִתְמַהְמֵהַּ וְגַם־צֵדָה לֹא־עָשׂוּ לָהֶם."

Matzah is the bread of poverty which the Israelites were made to eat as slaves. It is also the bread of freedom, reminding us of the haste in which the Israelites fled from Egypt. Its symbolism suggests that our experience has been one of enslavement *and* freedom, depending on our outlook. Transforming those things that enslave us is the journey that each individual must make if we are to develop: It is only once we let go of our enslavement that we can consider our freedom.

32

MAROR

מָרוֹר

Why do we eat these bitter herbs? Because the Egyptians embittered the lives of our ancestors in Egypt, as we read: "They made their lives bitter through hard labor with clay and bricks, and all kinds of work in the fields; for they were ruthless in the slave labor they imposed on them." (Ex. 1.14)

מָרוֹר זֶה שֶׁאָנוּ אוֹכְלִים עַל שׁוּם מָה? עַל שׁוּם שֶׁמֵּרְרוּ הַמִּצְרִים אֶת־חַיֵּי אֲבוֹתֵינוּ בְּמִצְרָיִם, שֶׁנֶּאֱמַר: "וַיְמָרְרוּ אֶת־חַיֵּיהֶם בַּעֲבֹדָה קָשָׁה, בְּחֹמֶר וּבִלְבֵנִים, וּבְכָל־עֲבֹדָה בַּשָּׂדֶה, אֵת כָּל־עֲבֹדָתָם אֲשֶׁר־עָבְדוּ בָהֶם בְּפָרֶךְ."

The bitter herbs are the taste of slavery—a reminder of the affliction that the Israelites endured in Egypt. They remind us of the inhumanity suffered not only by Jews but by other persecuted peoples around the world.

The maror is often illustrated as a stylized lettuce or as an artichoke. The Sephardic illumination opposite illustrates the tradition of the leader pointing to the maror rather than holding it up, a tradition more common among Ashkenazic Jews.

34

מָרוֹרָה

עַל שׁוּם מָה

שָׁמְּרְרוּ

אֶת חַיֵּי

בְּמִצְרַיִם

אֶת חַיֵּיהֶם

קָשָׁה בְּחֹמֶר

וּבְכֹל עֲבוֹדָה

כָּל יְבוּרָתָם

שֶׁאָם אוכ

עַל שום

הַמִּצְרִים

אֲבוֹתֵינו

שֶׁנּוּ יִמְרְרוּ

מֵעֲבוֹדָה

וְכֹל בֵּנ

מִשָּׂדֶה אֶת

אֲשֶׁר עָבְדוּ בָהֶם בְּפָרֶךְ

בְּכֹל דּוֹר וָדוֹר חַיָּיב אָדָם לִרְאוֹת

אֶת עַצְמוֹ כְּאִלּוּ הוּא יָצָא

מִמִּצְרַיִם שֶׁנֶּ׳ וְהִגַּדְתָּ לְבִנְךָ בַּיּוֹם הַהוּא לֵאמֹר בַּעֲבוּר

In Every Generation

בְּכָל־דּוֹר וָדוֹר

In every generation all individuals should regard themselves as if they personally had come out of Egypt, as we read, "You shall tell your child on that day: 'It is in commemoration of what God did for *me* when I came out of Egypt.'" For the Holy One, ever to be blessed, redeemed not only our ancestors, but us along with them, as it is said: "God led *us* out from there, so as to bring us into the land promised to our ancestors, and give it to us."

בְּכָל־דּוֹר וָדוֹר חַיָּב אָדָם לִרְאוֹת אֶת־עַצְמוֹ כְּאִלּוּ הוּא יָצָא מִמִּצְרַיִם, שֶׁנֶּאֱמַר, "וְהִגַּדְתָּ לְבִנְךָ בַּיּוֹם הַהוּא לֵאמֹר. בַּעֲבוּר זֶה עָשָׂה יְיָ לִי בְּצֵאתִי מִמִּצְרָיִם." לֹא אֶת־אֲבוֹתֵינוּ בִּלְבָד גָּאַל הַקָּדוֹשׁ בָּרוּךְ הוּא, אֶלָּא אַף אוֹתָנוּ גָּאַל עִמָּהֶם, שֶׁנֶּאֱמַר, "וְאוֹתָנוּ הוֹצִיא מִשָּׁם, לְמַעַן הָבִיא אֹתָנוּ, לָתֶת לָנוּ אֶת־הָאָרֶץ אֲשֶׁר נִשְׁבַּע לַאֲבֹתֵינוּ."

The cups are raised.

Therefore we should thank, bless, and praise beyond measure the One who performed all these wonders for our ancestors and for us; who led us from bondage to freedom, from sadness to joy, from mourning to celebration, from darkness to light, from servitude to redemption. Let us then sing to God a new song. Hallelujah!

לְפִיכָךְ אֲנַחְנוּ חַיָּבִים לְהוֹדוֹת לְהַלֵּל לְשַׁבֵּחַ לְפָאֵר לְרוֹמֵם לְהַדֵּר לְבָרֵךְ לְעַלֵּה וּלְקַלֵּס לְמִי שֶׁעָשָׂה לַאֲבוֹתֵינוּ וְלָנוּ אֶת־כָּל־הַנִּסִּים הָאֵלּוּ. הוֹצִיאָנוּ מֵעַבְדוּת לְחֵרוּת, מִיָּגוֹן לְשִׂמְחָה, וּמֵאֵבֶל לְיוֹם טוֹב, וּמֵאֲפֵלָה לְאוֹר גָּדוֹל, וּמִשִּׁעְבּוּד לִגְאֻלָּה. וְנֹאמַר לְפָנָיו שִׁירָה חֲדָשָׁה. הַלְלוּיָהּ.

The cups are put down.

There is a custom among Portuguese Jews to get up from the table at this point and pretend to be refugees from Egypt. In my family, true stories of being refugees are told by parents and grandparents. We therefore realize that the Seder is not just about retelling the story of the Exodus—it also encourages us to understand what it is like to be enslaved and to struggle for freedom. This is its most important lesson, and so we lift our glasses again and praise God's saving power.

HALLEL, FIRST PART

הַלֵּל, חֵלֶק רִאשׁוֹן

From Psalm 113

Hallelujah! Sing praises, you servants of God; praise the name of the Eternal One!

May God's name be blessed, now and forever. From the rising of the sun until its setting, may God's name be praised.

The Eternal One is exalted above all nations; God's glory above the heavens.

Who is like our Eternal God, enthroned so high,

Yet looking down upon the heavens and the earth! God lifts the needy from the dust, the wretched from squalor.

So as to seat them among nobles, the nobles of their people. Hallelujah!

הַלְלוּיָהּ! הַלְלוּ עַבְדֵי יְיָ, הַלְלוּ אֶת־שֵׁם יְיָ.
יְהִי שֵׁם יְיָ מְבֹרָךְ מֵעַתָּה וְעַד־עוֹלָם.

מִמִּזְרַח־שֶׁמֶשׁ עַד־מְבוֹאוֹ מְהֻלָּל שֵׁם יְיָ.

רָם עַל־כָּל־גּוֹיִם יְיָ, עַל הַשָּׁמַיִם כְּבוֹדוֹ.

מִי כַּיְיָ אֱלֹהֵינוּ, הַמַּגְבִּיהִי לָשָׁבֶת,
הַמַּשְׁפִּילִי לִרְאוֹת בַּשָּׁמַיִם וּבָאָרֶץ?
מְקִימִי מֵעָפָר דָּל, מֵאַשְׁפֹּת יָרִים אֶבְיוֹן.

לְהוֹשִׁיבִי עִם־נְדִיבִים, עִם נְדִיבֵי עַמּוֹ.

הַלְלוּיָהּ!

Psalm 114

When Israel went forth from Egypt, the House of Jacob from a foreign people,

Judah became God's sanctuary, Israel God's dominion.

The sea saw it and fled, the Jordan turned back;

The mountains skipped like rams, the hills like young lambs.

What frightens you, O sea, that you flee? O Jordan, that you turn back?

O mountains, that you skip like rams?
O hills, like young lambs?

Dance, O earth, before the Eternal One, before the God of Jacob,

Who turns the rock into a pool of water, the stony ground into a flowing spring.

בְּצֵאת יִשְׂרָאֵל מִמִּצְרָיִם, בֵּית יַעֲקֹב מֵעַם לֹעֵז,

הָיְתָה יְהוּדָה לְקָדְשׁוֹ, יִשְׂרָאֵל מַמְשְׁלוֹתָיו.

הַיָּם רָאָה וַיָּנֹס, הַיַּרְדֵּן יִסֹּב לְאָחוֹר.
הֶהָרִים רָקְדוּ כְאֵילִים, גְּבָעוֹת כִּבְנֵי־צֹאן.

מַה־לְּךָ הַיָּם כִּי תָנוּס, הַיַּרְדֵּן תִּסֹּב לְאָחוֹר.

הֶהָרִים תִּרְקְדוּ כְאֵילִים, גְּבָעוֹת כִּבְנֵי־צֹאן?

מִלִּפְנֵי אָדוֹן חוּלִי אָרֶץ, מִלִּפְנֵי אֱלוֹהַּ יַעֲקֹב.

הַהֹפְכִי הַצּוּר אֲגַם־מָיִם. חַלָּמִישׁ לְמַעְיְנוֹ־מָיִם.

37

THE SECOND CUP

We raise our cups in remembrance of the second promise of redemption, as it is said:

"And I will deliver you from their bondage." Blessed are You, our Eternal God, Ruler of the world, who has redeemed us and our ancestors from Egypt, and enabled us to reach this night, to celebrate our freedom by eating matzah and maror. Grant, Eternal God and God of our ancestors, that we may reach yet other holy days and festivals, living in peace, building Your City in gladness, and serving You in joy. Then we shall sing to You a new song of praise for our redemption from oppression and for our inner freedom. Blessed are You, O God, Redeemer of Israel.

Blessed are You, Eternal God, Ruler of the world, Creator of the fruit of the vine.

"וְהִצַּלְתִּי אֶתְכֶם מֵעֲבֹדָתָם." בָּרוּךְ אַתָּה יְיָ, אֱלֹהֵינוּ מֶלֶךְ הָעוֹלָם, אֲשֶׁר גְּאָלָנוּ וְגָאַל אֶת־אֲבוֹתֵינוּ מִמִּצְרַיִם, וְהִגִּיעָנוּ הַלַּיְלָה הַזֶּה, לֶאֱכָל־בּוֹ מַצָּה וּמָרוֹר. כֵּן, יְיָ אֱלֹהֵינוּ וֵאלֹהֵי אֲבוֹתֵינוּ, הַגִּיעֵנוּ לְמוֹעֲדִים וְלִרְגָלִים אֲחֵרִים, הַבָּאִים לִקְרָאתֵנוּ לְשָׁלוֹם, שְׂמֵחִים בְּבִנְיַן עִירֶךָ, וְשָׂשִׂים בַּעֲבוֹדָתֶךָ. וְנוֹדֶה לְךָ שִׁיר חָדָשׁ עַל־גְּאֻלָּתֵנוּ וְעַל־פְּדוּת נַפְשֵׁנוּ. בָּרוּךְ אַתָּה יְיָ, גָּאַל יִשְׂרָאֵל.

בָּרוּךְ אַתָּה יְיָ, אֱלֹהֵינוּ מֶלֶךְ הָעוֹלָם, בּוֹרֵא פְּרִי הַגָּפֶן.

All lean to the left and drink the Second Cup.

WASHING THE HANDS

רָחְצָה

Wash your hands and recite the following blessing:

Blessed are You, our Eternal God, Ruler of the world, who has sanctified our lives through Your commandments, and commanded us to perform the ritual washing of our hands.

בָּרוּךְ אַתָּה יְיָ, אֱלֹהֵינוּ מֶלֶךְ הָעוֹלָם, אֲשֶׁר קִדְּשָׁנוּ בְּמִצְוֹתָיו, וְצִוָּנוּ עַל נְטִילַת יָדָיִם.

BLESSING OVER THE MATZAH

מוֹצִיא מַצָּה

Blessed are You, our Eternal God, Ruler of the world who causes the earth to bring forth bread.

Blessed are You, our Eternal God, Ruler of the world, who has sanctified us by Your commandments, and enjoined us to eat unleavened bread.

בָּרוּךְ אַתָּה יְיָ, אֱלֹהֵינוּ מֶלֶךְ הָעוֹלָם, הַמּוֹצִיא לֶחֶם מִן הָאָרֶץ.

בָּרוּךְ אַתָּה יְיָ, אֱלֹהֵינוּ מֶלֶךְ הָעוֹלָם, אֲשֶׁר קִדְּשָׁנוּ בְּמִצְוֹתָיו וְצִוָּנוּ עַל אֲכִילַת מַצָּה.

All take a piece of matzah and, leaning to the left, eat it. The leader takes two pieces, one from the uppermost of the three matzot on the matzah plate, the other from what remains of the middle one, and eats them together.

MAROR

מָרוֹר

Before eating the maror, we dip it in the haroset which, by its appearance, reminds us of the clay and straw with which our ancestors were forced to make bricks for Pharaoh's building projects in Egypt. By its sweet taste, it softens, but does not remove, the bitter memory of their slavery.

All take a piece of maror, dip it in the haroset, and say:

Blessed are You, our Eternal God, Ruler of the world, who has sanctified us by Your commandments, and enjoined us to eat bitter herbs.

בָּרוּךְ אַתָּה יְיָ אֱלֹהֵינוּ מֶלֶךְ הָעוֹלָם, אֲשֶׁר קִדְּשָׁנוּ בְּמִצְוֹתָיו וְצִוָּנוּ עַל אֲכִילַת מָרוֹר.

The maror is eaten. Then all take another piece of maror and "sandwich" it between two pieces of matzah (the leader breaking these from the lowest of the three matzot on the matzah plate).

MATZAH AND MAROR

כּוֹרֵךְ

This is what Hillel used to do when the Temple still stood: he would combine the paschal lamb with unleavened bread and bitter herbs, and eat them together, to fulfil the verse: "With unleavened bread and bitter herbs shall they eat it."

כֵּן עָשָׂה הִלֵּל בִּזְמַן שֶׁבֵּית הַמִּקְדָּשׁ הָיָה קַיָּם. הָיָה כּוֹרֵךְ פֶּסַח מַצָּה וּמָרוֹר וְאוֹכֵל בְּיַחַד, לְקַיֵּם מַה שֶׁנֶּאֱמַר, עַל־מַצּוֹת וּמְרֹרִים יֹאכְלֻהוּ.

The "Hillel Sandwich" is eaten.

THE MEAL IS SERVED

שֻׁלְחָן עוֹרֵךְ

FINDING THE AFIKOMAN צָפוּן

At the end of the meal it is customary to invite the children to search for the Afikoman, the piece
of matzah that was hidden away at the beginning of the Seder, and to award a prize to the finder.
(Alternatively, the Afikoman may be hidden by the children and searched for by the leader, who,
failing to find it, has to ransom it from the children.)

The Afikoman is eaten.

The meaning of the word *afikoman* is uncertain, although it originates from the Greek
aphikomenos. The ancient rabbis thought it meant "dessert" or "after-dinner entertainment."
They instituted the eating of a piece of matzah at the end of the Seder as the Afikoman. A
modern scholar, Robert Eisler, believes that *aphikomenos* means "He who comes," referring
to the Messiah. Eisler's belief is echoed by the tradition of breaking off and hiding the
Afikoman, and then finding it. He comments that the Messiah is "broken off" from the
Jewish people: He exists but is as yet concealed. The Messiah's coming at the end of the
Seder will make the people whole.

In Jewish folklore, the Afikoman appears as a symbol of luck: In some Eastern communities,
people carried a piece of it around as protection against the evil eye. In others, it was customary
to preserve a piece of it between pages of the Haggadah for luck in the year ahead.

THANKSGIVING FOR THE MEAL בִּרְכַּת הַמָּזוֹן

The cups are refilled.
Psalm 126

A Song of Ascents.
שִׁיר הַמַּעֲלוֹת.

When God restored the exiles of Zion,
we felt as in a dream.
בְּשׁוּב יְיָ אֶת־שִׁיבַת צִיּוֹן הָיִינוּ כְּחֹלְמִים.

Our mouths were filled with laughter,
our tongues with joyful song.
אָז יִמָּלֵא שְׂחוֹק פִּינוּ וּלְשׁוֹנֵנוּ רִנָּה.

Then it was said among the nations:
"Their God has done great things for
them."
אָז יֹאמְרוּ בַגּוֹיִם, הִגְדִּיל יְיָ לַעֲשׂוֹת עִם־אֵלֶּה.

God *had* done great things for us, and
we rejoiced.
הִגְדִּיל יְיָ לַעֲשׂוֹת עִמָּנוּ, הָיִינוּ שְׂמֵחִים.

Once more, Eternal One, restore our
exiles, as streams revive the desert.
שׁוּבָה יְיָ אֶת־שְׁבִיתֵנוּ כַּאֲפִיקִים בַּנֶּגֶב.

Then those who sow in tears shall reap
in joy.
הַזֹּרְעִים בְּדִמְעָה בְּרִנָּה יִקְצֹרוּ.

Then those who go forth weeping, as
they bear their bags of seed, shall sing
for joy as they return, bringing home
their sheaves.
הָלוֹךְ יֵלֵךְ וּבָכֹה, נֹשֵׂא מֶשֶׁךְ־הַזָּרַע, בֹּא־יָבֹא בְרִנָּה נֹשֵׂא אֲלֻמֹּתָיו.

Leader

Let us praise God.

רַבּוֹתַי, נְבָרֵךְ.

All

Let God's name be praised, now and forever.

יְהִי שֵׁם יְיָ מְבֹרָךְ מֵעַתָּה וְעַד עוֹלָם.

Leader

Let us bless our God, of whose gifts we have eaten.

בִּרְשׁוּת רַבּוֹתַי נְבָרֵךְ אֱלֹהֵינוּ שֶׁאָכַלְנוּ מִשֶּׁלּוֹ.

All

Blessed be our God, of whose gifts we have eaten and by whose goodness we live.

בָּרוּךְ אֱלֹהֵינוּ שֶׁאָכַלְנוּ מִשֶּׁלּוֹ וּבְטוּבוֹ חָיִינוּ.

Leader

Blessed be God, and blessed be God's name.

בָּרוּךְ הוּא וּבָרוּךְ שְׁמוֹ.

Blessed are You, our Eternal God, Ruler of the world, by whose goodness the whole world is sustained. With grace, love and mercy You give food for all flesh, for Your love is unending. Through Your great goodness, we have never lacked our daily bread; may we never do so, for Your great name's sake. For You feed and nourish all, You are good to all, and provide enough for all Your creatures. Blessed are You, Eternal One, Sustainer of all.

בָּרוּךְ אַתָּה, יְיָ אֱלֹהֵינוּ, מֶלֶךְ הָעוֹלָם, הַזָּן אֶת־הָעוֹלָם כֻּלּוֹ בְּטוּבוֹ. בְּחֵן בְּחֶסֶד וּבְרַחֲמִים הוּא נוֹתֵן לֶחֶם לְכָל־בָּשָׂר, כִּי לְעוֹלָם חַסְדּוֹ. וּבְטוּבוֹ הַגָּדוֹל תָּמִיד לֹא־חָסַר לָנוּ, וְאַל יֶחְסַר־לָנוּ מָזוֹן לְעוֹלָם וָעֶד, בַּעֲבוּר שְׁמוֹ הַגָּדוֹל. כִּי הוּא זָן וּמְפַרְנֵס לַכֹּל וּמֵטִיב לַכֹּל וּמֵכִין מָזוֹן לְכָל־בְּרִיּוֹתָיו אֲשֶׁר בָּרָא. בָּרוּךְ אַתָּה יְיָ, הַזָּן אֶת־הַכֹּל.

We thank You, our Eternal God, for the pleasant, good and spacious land You gave our ancestors; for leading us out of Egypt, and redeeming us from the house of bondage; for the Covenant You have sealed into our hearts; for the Torah You have taught us, and the laws You have made known to us; for Your gracious gifts of life and love; and for the food with which You sustain us each and every day. For all these things, our Eternal God, we thank and bless You. May Your name be blessed continually by every living creature, as it is written: "When you have eaten and are satisfied, then bless your Eternal God for the good land that has been given you."

נוֹדֶה לְךָ, יְיָ אֱלֹהֵינוּ, עַל שֶׁהִנְחַלְתָּ לַאֲבוֹתֵינוּ אֶרֶץ חֶמְדָּה טוֹבָה וּרְחָבָה וְעַל שֶׁהוֹצֵאתָנוּ מֵאֶרֶץ מִצְרַיִם, וּפְדִיתָנוּ מִבֵּית עֲבָדִים, וְעַל בְּרִיתְךָ שֶׁחָתַמְתָּ בְּלִבֵּנוּ, וְעַל תּוֹרָתְךָ שֶׁלִּמַּדְתָּנוּ, וְעַל חֻקֶּיךָ שֶׁהוֹדַעְתָּנוּ, וְעַל חַיִּים חֵן וָחֶסֶד שֶׁחוֹנַנְתָּנוּ, וְעַל אֲכִילַת מָזוֹן שָׁאַתָּה זָן וּמְפַרְנֵס אוֹתָנוּ תָּמִיד בְּכָל־יוֹם וּבְכָל־עֵת וּבְכָל־שָׁעָה. וְעַל הַכֹּל, יְיָ אֱלֹהֵינוּ, אֲנַחְנוּ מוֹדִים לָךְ, וּמְבָרְכִים אוֹתָךְ, יִתְבָּרַךְ שִׁמְךָ בְּפִי כָּל־חַי תָּמִיד לְעוֹלָם וָעֶד, כַּכָּתוּב. "וְאָכַלְתָּ וְשָׂבָעְתָּ, וּבֵרַכְתָּ אֶת־יְיָ אֱלֹהֶיךָ עַל־הָאָרֶץ הַטֹּבָה אֲשֶׁר נָתַן־לָךְ."

Blessed are You, O God, for the land and for the food.

Have compassion, our Eternal God, on Your people Israel and on all the inhabitants of Your world. Our God and Creator, care for us, feed and sustain us, and may we soon be freed from all our afflictions. Let us never be dependent on gifts or loans from flesh and blood, but only on Your own, open and generous hand, so that we may never be embarrassed or ashamed.

בָּרוּךְ אַתָּה יְיָ, עַל־הָאָרֶץ וְעַל־הַמָּזוֹן.

רַחֵם, יְיָ אֱלֹהֵינוּ, עַל־יִשְׂרָאֵל עַמֶּךָ, וְעַל כָּל־יוֹשְׁבֵי תֵבֵל אַרְצֶךָ. אֱלֹהֵינוּ אָבִינוּ, רְעֵנוּ זוּנֵנוּ, פַּרְנְסֵנוּ וְכַלְכְּלֵנוּ וְהַרְוִיחֵנוּ, וְהַרְוַח־לָנוּ, יְיָ אֱלֹהֵינוּ, מְהֵרָה מִכָּל־צָרוֹתֵינוּ. וְנָא אַל־תַּצְרִיכֵנוּ, יְיָ אֱלֹהֵינוּ, לֹא לִידֵי מַתְּנַת בָּשָׂר וָדָם, וְלֹא לִידֵי הַלְוָאָתָם, כִּי אִם לְיָדְךָ הַמְּלֵאָה, הַפְּתוּחָה, הַקְּדוֹשָׁה וְהָרְחָבָה, שֶׁלֹּא נֵבוֹשׁ וְלֹא נִכָּלֵם לְעוֹלָם וָעֶד.

On a Sabbath

Eternal God, strengthen our resolve to obey Your commandments, and especially that of the seventh day, the great and holy Sabbath, that we may lovingly rest on it, and be refreshed by it, according to Your will. May it bring us true tranquillity, unmarred by sorrow or distress, and give us a foretaste of the consolation of Your people and the redemption of humanity; for You are the Author of redemption and the Source of consolation.

רְצֵה וְהַחֲלִיצֵנוּ, יְיָ אֱלֹהֵינוּ, בְּמִצְוֹתֶיךָ, וּבְמִצְוַת יוֹם הַשְּׁבִיעִי, הַשַּׁבָּת הַגָּדוֹל וְהַקָּדוֹשׁ הַזֶּה, לִשְׁבָּת־בּוֹ וְלָנוּחַ בּוֹ בְּאַהֲבָה כְּמִצְוַת רְצוֹנֶךָ. בִּרְצוֹנְךָ הָנִיחַ לָנוּ, יְיָ אֱלֹהֵינוּ, שֶׁלֹּא תְהִי צָרָה וְיָגוֹן וַאֲנָחָה בְּיוֹם מְנוּחָתֵנוּ. וְהַרְאֵנוּ, יְיָ אֱלֹהֵינוּ, בְּנֶחָמַת עַמֶּךָ, וּבְתִקּוּן עוֹלָמֶךָ, כִּי אַתָּה הוּא בַּעַל הַיְשׁוּעוֹת וּבַעַל הַנֶּחָמוֹת.

Our God and God of our ancestors, be mindful of Your people, the House of Israel, on this Festival of Unleavened Bread. May it bring us welfare and compassion, life and peace. At this season,

Remember us and be kind to us.
  Amen.

Consider us and bless us.
  Amen.

Deliver us and grant us life.
  Amen.

According to Your promise, be gracious and compassionate to us, and redeem us. To You do we look, for You are a gracious and compassionate God and Ruler.

אֱלֹהֵינוּ וֵאלֹהֵי אֲבוֹתֵינוּ, יַעֲלֶה וְיָבֹא, וְיֵרָאֶה וְיֵרָצֶה וְיִשָּׁמַע, וְיִפָּקֵד וְיִזָּכֵר זִכְרוֹנֵנוּ וְזִכְרוֹן כָּל־עַמְּךָ בֵּית יִשְׂרָאֵל לְפָנֶיךָ, לְטוֹבָה, לְחֵן, לְחֶסֶד וּלְרַחֲמִים, לְחַיִּים וּלְשָׁלוֹם בְּחַג הַמַּצּוֹת הַזֶּה.
זָכְרֵנוּ, יְיָ אֱלֹהֵינוּ, בּוֹ לְטוֹבָה.
אָמֵן.
וּפָקְדֵנוּ בוֹ לִבְרָכָה.
אָמֵן.
וְהוֹשִׁיעֵנוּ בוֹ לְחַיִּים.
אָמֵן.
וּבִדְבַר יְשׁוּעָה וְרַחֲמִים, חוּס וְחָנֵּנוּ, וְרַחֵם עָלֵינוּ וְהוֹשִׁיעֵנוּ, כִּי אֵל מֶלֶךְ חַנּוּן וְרַחוּם אָתָּה.

O let Jerusalem be built in our time: the City of Holiness. Blessed are You, O God, who in compassion will build Jerusalem.
  Amen.

Blessed are You, our Eternal God, Ruler of the world, our caring God and Sovereign, mighty Creator and Redeemer, the Holy One of Jacob and the Shepherd of Israel, good and beneficent to all. Show us Your love and kindness in the future as in the past. Grant us grace and compassion, freedom and deliverance, prosperity and blessing, redemption and consolation, sustenance, life, and peace; may we never lack all that we need for our good.

May the Merciful One rule over us forever.
  Amen.

May the Merciful One be blessed in heaven and on earth.
  Amen.

May the Merciful One be praised by all generations; may God be extolled and glorified by us forever.
  Amen.

May the Merciful One bless this house, and this table at which we have eaten.
  Amen.

May the Merciful One send us Elijah, the prophet, with good tidings of deliverance and consolation.
  Amen.

May the Merciful One bless us and all our dear ones. As our ancestors Abraham, Isaac and Jacob, Sarah, Rebekah, Rachel, and Leah, were blessed in all things, so may we be blessed, one and all; and let us say:
  Amen.

May our merit be invoked on high, leading to enduring peace. May we receive blessings from the Eternal One, and kindness from the God of our salvation, and earn the sympathy and trust of God and all people.

וּבְנֵה יְרוּשָׁלַיִם, עִיר הַקֹּדֶשׁ, בִּמְהֵרָה בְיָמֵינוּ. בָּרוּךְ אַתָּה יְיָ, בּוֹנֶה בְרַחֲמָיו יְרוּשָׁלָיִם.
אָמֵן.

בָּרוּךְ אַתָּה יְיָ, אֱלֹהֵינוּ מֶלֶךְ הָעוֹלָם, הָאֵל אָבִינוּ, מַלְכֵּנוּ, אַדִּירֵנוּ, בּוֹרְאֵנוּ, גּוֹאֲלֵנוּ, יוֹצְרֵנוּ, קְדוֹשֵׁנוּ קְדוֹשׁ יַעֲקֹב, רוֹעֵנוּ, רוֹעֵה יִשְׂרָאֵל, הַמֶּלֶךְ הַטּוֹב, וְהַמֵּטִיב לַכֹּל, שֶׁבְּכָל־יוֹם וָיוֹם הוּא הֵטִיב, הוּא מֵטִיב, הוּא יֵטִיב לָנוּ; הוּא גְמָלָנוּ, הוּא גוֹמְלֵנוּ, הוּא יִגְמְלֵנוּ לָעַד, לְחֵן, לְחֶסֶד וּלְרַחֲמִים וּלְרֶוַח, הַצָּלָה וְהַצְלָחָה בְּרָכָה וִישׁוּעָה, נֶחָמָה, פַּרְנָסָה וְכַלְכָּלָה, וְרַחֲמִים וְחַיִּים וְשָׁלוֹם וְכָל־טוֹב; וּמִכָּל־טוֹב לְעוֹלָם אַל יְחַסְּרֵנוּ.

הָרַחֲמָן הוּא יִמְלֹךְ עָלֵינוּ לְעוֹלָם וָעֶד.
אָמֵן.

הָרַחֲמָן הוּא יִתְבָּרַךְ בַּשָּׁמַיִם וּבָאָרֶץ.
אָמֵן.

הָרַחֲמָן הוּא יִשְׁתַּבַּח לְדוֹר דּוֹרִים, וְיִתְפָּאַר בָּנוּ לְנֶצַח נְצָחִים, וְיִתְהַדַּר בָּנוּ לָעַד וּלְעוֹלְמֵי עוֹלָמִים.
אָמֵן.

הָרַחֲמָן הוּא יִשְׁלַח בְּרָכָה מְרֻבָּה בַּבַּיִת הַזֶּה וְעַל שֻׁלְחָן זֶה שֶׁאָכַלְנוּ עָלָיו.
אָמֵן.

הָרַחֲמָן הוּא יִשְׁלַח לָנוּ אֶת־אֵלִיָּהוּ הַנָּבִיא זָכוּר לַטּוֹב, וִיבַשֶּׂר־לָנוּ בְּשׂוֹרוֹת טוֹבוֹת, יְשׁוּעוֹת וְנֶחָמוֹת.
אָמֵן.

הָרַחֲמָן הוּא יְבָרֵךְ אוֹתָנוּ וְאֶת־כָּל־אֲשֶׁר לָנוּ כְּמוֹ שֶׁנִּתְבָּרְכוּ אֲבוֹתֵינוּ אַבְרָהָם, יִצְחָק וְיַעֲקֹב וְאִמּוֹתֵינוּ שָׂרָה, רִבְקָה, רָחֵל וְלֵאָה, בַּכֹּל מִכֹּל כֹּל, כֵּן יְבָרֵךְ אוֹתָנוּ כֻּלָּנוּ יַחַד בִּבְרָכָה שְׁלֵמָה, וְנֹאמַר.
אָמֵן.

בַּמָּרוֹם יְלַמְּדוּ עֲלֵיהֶם וְעָלֵינוּ זְכוּת שֶׁתְּהִי לְמִשְׁמֶרֶת שָׁלוֹם. וְנִשָּׂא בְרָכָה מֵאֵת יְיָ, וּצְדָקָה מֵאֱלֹהֵי יִשְׁעֵנוּ, וְנִמְצָא חֵן וְשֵׂכֶל טוֹב בְּעֵינֵי אֱלֹהִים וְאָדָם.

On a Sabbath

May the Merciful One grant us perfect Sabbath rest and peace in the life of eternity. Amen.

הָרַחֲמָן הוּא יַנְחִילֵנוּ יוֹם שֶׁכֻּלוֹ שַׁבָּת וּמְנוּחָה לְחַיֵּי הָעוֹלָמִים. אָמֵן.

_____

May the Merciful One grant us an eternal day of perfect joy. Amen.

הָרַחֲמָן הוּא יַנְחִילֵנוּ יוֹם שֶׁכֻּלוֹ טוֹב. אָמֵן.

May the Merciful One make us worthy to witness the Messianic Age and the Life of the World to Come.

הָרַחֲמָן הוּא יְזַכֵּנוּ לִימוֹת הַמָּשִׁיחַ וּלְחַיֵּי הָעוֹלָם הַבָּא.

God is a tower of righteous victories for the one who rules in God's name, an eternal provider of convenantal love for the one God anointed, David and his seed.

מִגְדּוֹל יְשׁוּעוֹת מַלְכּוֹ וְעֹשֶׂה חֶסֶד לִמְשִׁיחוֹ לְדָוִד וּלְזַרְעוֹ עַד־עוֹלָם.

May God who causes peace to reign in the heavens above grant peace to us, to all Israel, and to all the world.

עֹשֶׂה שָׁלוֹם בִּמְרוֹמָיו, הוּא יַעֲשֶׂה שָׁלוֹם עָלֵינוּ וְעַל כָּל־יִשְׂרָאֵל וְעַל כָּל־בְּנֵי אָדָם.

May God give strength to this people; may God bless this people with peace.

יְיָ עֹז לְעַמּוֹ יִתֵּן; יְיָ יְבָרֵךְ אֶת־עַמּוֹ בַשָּׁלוֹם.

THE THIRD CUP

כּוֹס שֶׁל בְּרָכָה

We raise our cups in remembrance of the third promise of redemption, as it is said:

I will redeem you with an outstretched arm and with great acts of judgment.

וְגָאַלְתִּי אֶתְכֶם בִּזְרוֹעַ נְטוּיָה וּבִשְׁפָטִים גְּדֹלִים.

Blessed are You, our Eternal God, Ruler of the world, Creator of the fruit of the vine.

בָּרוּךְ אַתָּה יְיָ, אֱלֹהֵינוּ מֶלֶךְ הָעוֹלָם, בּוֹרֵא פְּרִי הַגָּפֶן.

All lean to the left and drink the Third Cup.

Pour the Fourth Cup and pour the cup of Elijah, the Prophet. Open the door and say:

Behold, I will send you Elijah the prophet before the coming of the great and awesome day of God; and he will turn the hearts of parents to their children, and the hearts of children to their parents.

הִנֵּה אָנֹכִי שֹׁלֵחַ לָכֶם אֵת אֵלִיָּה הַנָּבִיא לִפְנֵי בּוֹא יוֹם יְיָ הַגָּדוֹל וְהַנּוֹרָא; וְהֵשִׁיב לֵב־אָבוֹת עַל־בָּנִים, וְלֵב בָּנִים עַל־אֲבוֹתָם.

Pouring the Fifth Cup, Elijah's cup, symbolizes God's fifth promise: "I will bring you into the land."

Elijah, whose coming is said to herald the Messianic Age, is expected at three particular occasions: at Havdalah (the conclusion of the Sabbath), at the circumcision of an eight-day-old male baby, and at the Passover Seder. All are times of special power: A Sabbath without end would be the start of the Messianic Age, every child born has the potential to bring about that Messianic Age, and because Passover celebrates freedom, it is a time of hope for the future—we open the door and fill Elijah's cup in the belief that the Messianic Age will come. Only when it comes will we drink from the cup.

There is a custom (said to have been introduced by Rabbi Naftali of Ropschitz, a Hasid who lived in Galicia during the 18th century), that each participant at the Seder pours wine from his or her glass into Elijah's cup. This is symbolic, too: We all need to make a personal contribution to help bring about the Messianic Age.

"Pour out Your wrath upon those who do not know You and upon the governments which do not call upon Your name. For they have devoured Jacob and laid waste his dwelling place." (Ps. 79.6-7)

שְׁפֹךְ חֲמָתְךָ אֶל־הַגּוֹיִם אֲשֶׁר לֹא־יְדָעוּךָ וְעַל מַמְלָכוֹת אֲשֶׁר בְּשִׁמְךָ לֹא קָרָאוּ: כִּי אָכַל אֶת־יַעֲקֹב וְאֶת־נָוֵהוּ הֵשַׁמּוּ.

"Pour out Your fury upon them, let the fierceness of Your anger overtake them." (Ps. 69.25)

שְׁפָךְ־עֲלֵיהֶם זַעְמֶךָ וַחֲרוֹן אַפְּךָ יַשִּׂיגֵם.

"Pursue them in indignation and destroy them from under Your heavens." (Lam. 3.66)

תִּרְדֹּף בְּאַף וְתַשְׁמִידֵם מִתַּחַת שְׁמֵי יְיָ.

On the day before Pesach, 1943, German troops entered the Warsaw ghetto to deport the inhabitants to Treblinka. Jewish resistance fighters in the ghetto forced the Germans to withdraw, but they knew that the troops would soon return. That night, according to the diary of Tuvia Borzykowski, a partisan fighter during World War II, the reading of the Haggadah was punctuated by gunfire and bursting shells. The Jews wept as the rabbi intoned: "Pour out Your wrath upon those who do not know You."

HALLEL, SECOND PART

Close the door and continue the Hallel Psalms.
Psalm 117

הַלֵּל, חֵלֶק שֵׁנִי

הַלְלוּ אֶת־יְיָ כָּל־גּוֹיִם, שַׁבְּחוּהוּ
כָּל־הָאֻמִּים.
כִּי גָבַר עָלֵינוּ חַסְדּוֹ, וֶאֱמֶת־יְיָ
לְעוֹלָם. הַלְלוּיָהּ.

Praise the Eternal One, all you nations!
Extol God, all you peoples!
For great is God's love for us;
God's faithfulness endures for ever.
Hallelujah!

From Psalm 118

Give thanks to the Eternal One, for it is good;
God's love endures forever.

הוֹדוּ לַיְיָ כִּי־טוֹב, כִּי לְעוֹלָם חַסְדּוֹ.

Let Israel now say: God's love endures forever.

יֹאמַר־נָא יִשְׂרָאֵל, כִּי לְעוֹלָם חַסְדּוֹ.

Let the House of Aaron now say: God's love
endures forever.

יֹאמְרוּ־נָא בֵית־אַהֲרֹן, כִּי לְעוֹלָם חַסְדּוֹ.

Let all who fear the Eternal One now say: God's
love endures forever.

יֹאמְרוּ־נָא יִרְאֵי יְיָ, כִּי לְעוֹלָם חַסְדּוֹ.

In my distress I called to God, who answered me
and set me free.

מִן־הַמֵּצַר קָרָאתִי יָּהּ; עָנָנִי בַמֶּרְחָב יָהּ.

God is with me, I shall not fear;
what can people do to me?

יְיָ לִי, לֹא אִירָא; מַה־יַּעֲשֶׂה לִי אָדָם?

With God as my Helper, I can face my enemies.
It is better to trust in God than to rely on human
help.

יְיָ לִי בְּעֹזְרָי, וַאֲנִי אֶרְאֶה בְשֹׂנְאָי.
טוֹב לַחֲסוֹת בַּיְיָ מִבְּטֹחַ בָּאָדָם.

It is better to trust in God than to rely on nobles.

טוֹב לַחֲסוֹת בַּיְיָ מִבְּטֹחַ בִּנְדִיבִים.

Eternal, my strength and my shield; you have
become my salvation.

עָזִּי וְזִמְרָת יָהּ, וַיְהִי־לִי לִישׁוּעָה.

Hear! Glad songs of triumph in the tents of the
righteous! God's right hand is mighty!

קוֹל רִנָּה וִישׁוּעָה בְּאָהֳלֵי צַדִּיקִים! יְמִין יְיָ עֹשָׂה
חָיִל!

God's right hand is exalted; God's right hand is
mighty!

יְמִין יְיָ רוֹמֵמָה; יְמִין יְיָ עֹשָׂה חָיִל.

I shall not die, but live, and proclaim the deeds
of God.

לֹא־אָמוּת, כִּי־אֶחְיֶה, וַאֲסַפֵּר מַעֲשֵׂי יָהּ.

God has chastened me severely, but not abandoned me to death.

Open for me the gates of righteousness, that I may enter them and give thanks.

This is the gate of God: the righteous shall enter it.

I give You thanks, because You have answered me, and have been my salvation.

The stone which the builders rejected has become the chief cornerstone.

This is God's doing; it is marvelous in our eyes.

This is the day that God has made; let us delight and rejoice in it.

O God, save us!
O God, save us!
O God, prosper us!
O God, prosper us!

Blessed be the one who comes in the name of God; we bless you from the house of God.

You are my God, and I will thank You; You are my God, I will exalt You.

Give thanks to the Eternal One, who is good; whose love endures forever.

Let all creation praise You, Eternal God. Let all the faithful and righteous, who do Your will, together with the whole House of Israel, Your people, thank, bless, and extol You in joyful song, and proclaim Your holiness and sovereignty, our Ruler. For it is good to thank You, and pleasant to sing to You, the everlasting God. We praise You, Eternal Ruler, forever to be acclaimed in songs of praise.

יַסֹּר יִסְּרַנִּי יָּהּ, וְלַמָּוֶת לֹא נְתָנָנִי.

פִּתְחוּ־לִי שַׁעֲרֵי־צֶדֶק, אָבֹא־בָם אוֹדֶה יָהּ.

זֶה־הַשַּׁעַר לַיְיָ: צַדִּיקִים יָבֹאוּ בוֹ.

אוֹדְךָ כִּי עֲנִיתָנִי, וַתְּהִי־לִי לִישׁוּעָה.

אֶבֶן מָאֲסוּ הַבּוֹנִים הָיְתָה לְרֹאשׁ פִּנָּה.

מֵאֵת יְיָ הָיְתָה זֹּאת, הִיא נִפְלָאת בְּעֵינֵינוּ.

זֶה־הַיּוֹם עָשָׂה יְיָ, נָגִילָה וְנִשְׂמְחָה בוֹ.

אָנָּא יְיָ, הוֹשִׁיעָה נָּא.
אָנָּא יְיָ, הוֹשִׁיעָה נָּא.
אָנָּא יְיָ, הַצְלִיחָה נָּא.
אָנָּא יְיָ, הַצְלִיחָה נָּא.

בָּרוּךְ הַבָּא בְּשֵׁם יְיָ, בֵּרַכְנוּכֶם מִבֵּית יְיָ.

אֵלִי אַתָּה וְאוֹדֶךָּ, אֱלֹהַי אֲרוֹמְמֶךָּ.

הוֹדוּ לַיְיָ כִּי־טוֹב, כִּי לְעוֹלָם חַסְדּוֹ.

יְהַלְלוּךָ, יְיָ אֱלֹהֵינוּ, כָּל־מַעֲשֶׂיךָ, וַחֲסִידֶיךָ צַדִּיקִים עוֹשֵׂי רְצוֹנֶךָ, וְכָל־עַמְּךָ בֵּית־יִשְׂרָאֵל, בְּרִנָּה יוֹדוּ וִיבָרְכוּ, וִישַׁבְּחוּ וִיפָאֲרוּ, וִירוֹמְמוּ וְיַעֲרִיצוּ, וְיַקְדִּישׁוּ וְיַמְלִיכוּ אֶת־שִׁמְךָ, מַלְכֵּנוּ. כִּי לְךָ טוֹב לְהוֹדוֹת, וּלְשִׁמְךָ נָאֶה לְזַמֵּר, כִּי מֵעוֹלָם וְעַד עוֹלָם אַתָּה אֵל. בָּרוּךְ אַתָּה יְיָ, מֶלֶךְ מְהֻלָּל בַּתִּשְׁבָּחוֹת.

From Psalm 136

Give thanks to the Eternal One, who is good;	הוֹדוּ לַייָ כִּי־טוֹב,
God's love endures forever.	כִּי לְעוֹלָם חַסְדּוֹ.
Give thanks to the God above all gods;	הוֹדוּ לֵאלֹהֵי הָאֱלֹהִים,
God's love endures forever.	כִּי לְעוֹלָם חַסְדּוֹ.
Give thanks to the Power above all powers;	הוֹדוּ לַאֲדֹנֵי הָאֲדֹנִים,
God's love endures forever.	כִּי לְעוֹלָם חַסְדּוֹ.
To the One who alone performs great wonders;	לְעֹשֵׂה נִפְלָאוֹת גְּדֹלוֹת לְבַדּוֹ,
whose love endures forever.	כִּי לְעוֹלָם חַסְדּוֹ.
Who in wisdom made the heavens;	לְעֹשֵׂה הַשָּׁמַיִם בִּתְבוּנָה,
God's love endures forever.	כִּי לְעוֹלָם חַסְדּוֹ.
Who spread forth the earth above the waters;	לְרוֹקַע הָאָרֶץ עַל־הַמָּיִם,
God's love endures forever.	כִּי לְעוֹלָם חַסְדּוֹ.
Who created the great lights;	לְעֹשֵׂה אוֹרִים גְּדֹלִים,
God's love endures forever.	כִּי לְעוֹלָם חַסְדּוֹ.
The sun to rule by day;	אֶת־הַשֶּׁמֶשׁ לְמֶמְשֶׁלֶת בַּיּוֹם,
God's love endures forever.	כִּי לְעוֹלָם חַסְדּוֹ.
The moon and stars to rule by night;	אֶת־הַיָּרֵחַ וְכוֹכָבִים לְמֶמְשְׁלוֹת בַּלָּיְלָה,
God's love endures forever.	כִּי לְעוֹלָם חַסְדּוֹ.
Who brought Israel out of Egypt;	וַיּוֹצֵא יִשְׂרָאֵל מִמִּצְרָיִם,
God's love endures forever.	כִּי לְעוֹלָם חַסְדּוֹ.
With mighty hand and outstretched arm;	בְּיָד חֲזָקָה וּבִזְרוֹעַ נְטוּיָה,
God's love endures forever.	כִּי לְעוֹלָם חַסְדּוֹ.
Who divided the Red Sea in two;	לְגֹזֵר יַם־סוּף לִגְזָרִים,
God's love endures forever.	כִּי לְעוֹלָם חַסְדּוֹ.
And enabled Israel to pass through it;	וְהֶעֱבִיר יִשְׂרָאֵל בְּתוֹכוֹ,
God's love endures forever.	כִּי לְעוֹלָם חַסְדּוֹ.
And led the people through the wilderness;	לְמוֹלִיךְ עַמּוֹ בַּמִּדְבָּר,
God's love endures forever.	כִּי לְעוֹלָם חַסְדּוֹ.
Who remembered us in our deep distress;	שֶׁבְּשִׁפְלֵנוּ זָכַר־לָנוּ,
God's love endures forever.	כִּי לְעוֹלָם חַסְדּוֹ.
And delivered us from our enemies;	וַיִּפְרְקֵנוּ מִצָּרֵינוּ,
God's love endures forever.	כִּי לְעוֹלָם חַסְדּוֹ.
Who gives food for all creatures;	נוֹתֵן לֶחֶם לְכָל־בָּשָׂר,
God's love endures forever.	כִּי לְעוֹלָם חַסְדּוֹ.
O give thanks to the God of heaven;	הוֹדוּ לְאֵל הַשָּׁמָיִם,
God's love endures forever.	כִּי לְעוֹלָם חַסְדּוֹ.

NISHMAT

Let all the living give praise to Your name, our Eternal God;

 Let every human spirit acclaim Your majesty forever.

Through all eternity You are God; we have no Ruler but You,

 No other Helper or Redeemer to sustain and pity us in time of trouble and distress.

God of all ages, God of all creatures, Guide of all generations: You are greatly to be praised.

 You guide the world with constant love, Your creatures with tender care.

You neither slumber nor sleep;

 You awaken the sleeping and rouse those who slumber.

You give speech to the silent, freedom to the enslaved, support to the falling, justice to the oppressed.

 To You alone we give thanks.

Yet though our mouths should overflow with song as the sea,

Our tongues with melody as the roaring waves,

And our lips with praise as heaven's wide expanse;

Though our eyes should shine as the sun and moon,

Our arms extend like eagles' wings,

And our feet speed swiftly as hinds—

Still we could not fully thank You,

Eternal God and God of our ancestors,

Or praise Your name enough,

For Your infinite kindness to our ancestors and to us.

 From Egypt You redeemed us, Eternal God, and from the house of bondage you released us.

 In times of famine You have sustained us,

 In times of plenty provided for us.

נִשְׁמַת

נִשְׁמַת כָּל־חַי תְּבָרֵךְ אֶת־שִׁמְךָ יְיָ אֱלֹהֵינוּ,

וְרוּחַ כָּל־בָּשָׂר תְּפָאֵר וּתְרוֹמֵם זִכְרְךָ, מַלְכֵּנוּ, תָּמִיד. מִן־הָעוֹלָם וְעַד־הָעוֹלָם אַתָּה אֵל, וּמִבַּלְעָדֶיךָ אֵין לָנוּ מֶלֶךְ,

גּוֹאֵל וּמוֹשִׁיעַ, פּוֹדֶה וּמַצִּיל וּמְפַרְנֵס וּמְרַחֵם בְּכָל־עֵת צָרָה וְצוּקָה, אֵין לָנוּ מֶלֶךְ אֶלָּא אַתָּה. אֱלֹהֵי הָרִאשׁוֹנִים וְהָאַחֲרוֹנִים, אֱלוֹהַּ כָּל־בְּרִיּוֹת, אֲדוֹן כָּל־תּוֹלָדוֹת, הַמְהֻלָּל בְּרֹב הַתִּשְׁבָּחוֹת, הַמְנַהֵג עוֹלָמוֹ בְּחֶסֶד וּבְרִיּוֹתָיו בְּרַחֲמִים. וַיְיָ לֹא־יָנוּם וְלֹא־יִישָׁן,

הַמְעוֹרֵר יְשֵׁנִים, וְהַמֵּקִיץ נִרְדָּמִים,

וְהַמֵּשִׂיחַ אִלְּמִים, וְהַמַּתִּיר אֲסוּרִים, וְהַסּוֹמֵךְ נוֹפְלִים, וְהַזּוֹקֵף כְּפוּפִים,

לְךָ לְבַדְּךָ אֲנַחְנוּ מוֹדִים.

אִלּוּ פִינוּ מָלֵא שִׁירָה כַּיָּם,

וּלְשׁוֹנֵנוּ רִנָּה כַּהֲמוֹן גַּלָּיו,

וְשִׂפְתוֹתֵינוּ שֶׁבַח כְּמֶרְחֲבֵי רָקִיעַ,

וְעֵינֵינוּ מְאִירוֹת כַּשֶּׁמֶשׁ וְכַיָּרֵחַ,

וְיָדֵינוּ פְרוּשׂוֹת כְּנִשְׁרֵי שָׁמָיִם, וְרַגְלֵינוּ קַלּוֹת כָּאַיָּלוֹת - אֵין אֲנַחְנוּ מַסְפִּיקִים לְהוֹדוֹת לָךְ, יְיָ אֱלֹהֵינוּ וֵאלֹהֵי אֲבוֹתֵינוּ, וּלְבָרֵךְ אֶת־שִׁמְךָ עַל־אַחַת מֵאֶלֶף אֶלֶף אַלְפֵי אֲלָפִים וְרִבֵּי רְבָבוֹת פְּעָמִים, הַטּוֹבוֹת שֶׁעָשִׂיתָ עִם־אֲבוֹתֵינוּ וְעִמָּנוּ. מִמִּצְרַיִם גְּאַלְתָּנוּ, יְיָ אֱלֹהֵינוּ, וּמִבֵּית עֲבָדִים פְּדִיתָנוּ.

בְּרָעָב זַנְתָּנוּ, וּבְשָׂבָע כִּלְכַּלְתָּנוּ.

From the sword You have delivered us,
From plagues and diseases rescued us.

Until this day Your mercy has upheld us,
Your love has never failed us.
Do not forsake us, Eternal God; remain our help
forever.

And so the limbs You have formed in us,
The spirit You have breathed into us,
The tongue You have set in our mouths –
All shall unite to thank and bless,
Praise and exalt You,
And proclaim Your holiness and sovereignty.

Every mouth shall acknowledge You;
Every tongue swear allegiance to You;
Every knee shall bend to You;
Every body bow down to You;
Every heart shall revere You;
And every fiber of our being shall sing Your praise.

For thus it is written: "All my bones
shall say: 'Who is like You, O God?'"
Who indeed is like You?
Who is Your equal?
Who can compare with You,
O great and mighty, awesome and exalted God,
Creator of heaven and earth?

Therefore we praise You, proclaim Your glory, and
bless Your holy name, as it is said:
"Bless the Eternal One, my soul;
Let all that is within me bless God's holy name."

YISHTABACH

O great and holy God and Ruler,
Your name be praised forevermore in heaven and
on earth.
To You, our God and God of our ancestors,
Let hymns and psalms be sung unceasingly.
All might and majesty, all victory and greatness,
All glory, holiness, and sovereignty are Yours. To
You all thanks are due, all praise belongs, from
now until the end of time.
Accept then our reverence, our gratitude, our songs
of praise,
Our Eternal God and Ruler, Author of wonders,
Source of the life of all worlds.

מֵחֶרֶב הִצַּלְתָּנוּ, וּמִדֶּבֶר מִלַּטְתָּנוּ, וּמֵחֳלָיִם רָעִים
וְנֶאֱמָנִים דִּלִּיתָנוּ.
עַד־הֵנָּה עֲזָרוּנוּ רַחֲמֶיךָ, וְלֹא־עֲזָבוּנוּ חֲסָדֶיךָ,
וְאַל־תִּטְּשֵׁנוּ, יְיָ אֱלֹהֵינוּ, לָנֶצַח.

עַל־כֵּן אֵבָרִים שֶׁפִּלַּגְתָּ בָּנוּ,
וְרוּחַ וּנְשָׁמָה שֶׁנָּפַחְתָּ בְּאַפֵּינוּ,
וְלָשׁוֹן אֲשֶׁר שַׂמְתָּ בְּפִינוּ-
הֵן הֵם יוֹדוּ וִיבָרְכוּ, וִישַׁבְּחוּ וִיפָאֲרוּ, וִירוֹמְמוּ
וְיַעֲרִיצוּ, וְיַקְדִּישׁוּ וְיַמְלִיכוּ אֶת־שִׁמְךָ, מַלְכֵּנוּ.

כִּי כָל־פֶּה לְךָ יוֹדֶה,
וְכָל־לָשׁוֹן לְךָ תִשָּׁבַע,
וְכָל־בֶּרֶךְ לְךָ תִכְרַע, וְכָל־קוֹמָה לְפָנֶיךָ תִשְׁתַּחֲוֶה,
וְכָל־לְבָבוֹת יִירָאוּךָ,
וְכָל־קֶרֶב וּכְלָיוֹת יְזַמְּרוּ לִשְׁמֶךָ,
כַּדָּבָר שֶׁכָּתוּב: "כָּל עַצְמוֹתַי תֹּאמַרְנָה:
יְיָ, מִי כָמוֹךָ?" מִי יִדְמֶה־לָךְ?
וּמִי יִשְׁוֶה לָּךְ? וּמִי יַעֲרָךְ־לָךְ?
הָאֵל הַגָּדוֹל, הַגִּבּוֹר וְהַנּוֹרָא, אֵל עֶלְיוֹן,
קֹנֵה שָׁמַיִם וָאָרֶץ?

נְהַלֶּלְךָ וּנְשַׁבֵּחֲךָ וּנְפָאֶרְךָ,
וּנְבָרֵךְ אֶת־שֵׁם קָדְשֶׁךָ, כָּאָמוּר:
"בָּרְכִי נַפְשִׁי אֶת־יְיָ, וְכָל־קְרָבַי אֶת־שֵׁם קָדְשׁוֹ."

יִשְׁתַּבַּח

יִשְׁתַּבַּח שִׁמְךָ לָעַד מַלְכֵּנוּ,
הָאֵל הַמֶּלֶךְ הַגָּדוֹל וְהַקָּדוֹשׁ בַּשָּׁמַיִם וּבָאָרֶץ.

כִּי לְךָ נָאֶה, יְיָ אֱלֹהֵינוּ וֵאלֹהֵי אֲבוֹתֵינוּ,
שִׁיר וּשְׁבָחָה, הַלֵּל וְזִמְרָה, עֹז וּמֶמְשָׁלָה,
נֶצַח, גְּדֻלָּה וּגְבוּרָה, תְּהִלָּה וְתִפְאֶרֶת, קְדֻשָּׁה
וּמַלְכוּת, בְּרָכוֹת וְהוֹדָאוֹת, מֵעַתָּה וְעַד־עוֹלָם.

בָּרוּךְ אַתָּה יְיָ, אֵל מֶלֶךְ גָּדוֹל בַּתִּשְׁבָּחוֹת,
אֵל הַהוֹדָאוֹת, אֲדוֹן הַנִּפְלָאוֹת,
הַבּוֹחֵר בְּשִׁירֵי זִמְרָה, מֶלֶךְ אֵל חֵי הָעוֹלָמִים.

THE FOURTH CUP

כּוֹס רְבִיעִי

We raise our cups in remembrance of the fourth promise of redemption, as it is said:

"I will take you as My people, and I will be your God."

Blessed are You, Our Eternal God, Ruler of the world, Creator of the fruit of the vine.

וְלָקַחְתִּי אֶתְכֶם לִי לְעָם, וְהָיִיתִי לָכֶם לֵאלֹהִים.
בָּרוּךְ אַתָּה יְיָ, אֱלֹהֵינוּ מֶלֶךְ הָעוֹלָם, בּוֹרֵא פְּרִי הַגָּפֶן.

All lean to the left and drink the Fourth Cup.

CONCLUDING PRAYER

סִיוּם

The order of the Passover has been completed according to its precepts, with all its customs and ordinances. Just as it has been granted us to perform it now, so may we be worthy to fulfill it in the future. Pure One, dwelling on high, raise up to Yourself a congregation without number. Bring us back soon the plants of Your vineyard, redeemed into Zion with joyful song.

חֲסַל סִדּוּר פֶּסַח כְּהִלְכָתוֹ, כְּכָל־מִשְׁפָּטוֹ וְחֻקָּתוֹ. כַּאֲשֶׁר זָכִינוּ לְסַדֵּר אוֹתוֹ, כֵּן נִזְכֶּה לַעֲשׂוֹתוֹ. זָךְ שׁוֹכֵן מְעוֹנָה, קוֹמֵם קְהַל עֲדַת מִי מָנָה. בְּקָרוֹב נַהֵל נִטְעֵי כַנָּה.

פְּדוּיִם לְצִיּוֹן בְּרִנָּה.

NEXT YEAR IN JERUSALEM!

לְשָׁנָה הַבָּאָה בִּירוּשָׁלָיִם !

In addition to being capital of the Jewish state and a holy place for Moslems and Christians, Jerusalem is considered by the Jewish people to be their Holy City. It represents the spiritual ideal of a heavenly place where tranquillity and harmony reign. As Jews, it is our duty to work toward a peaceful Jerusalem for all, and we pray to be in such a place.

Tonight, as in every generation, we have recalled how the Israelites were freed from slavery in Egypt. We have recalled the significance of Passover in the consciousness of the Jewish people, from the Temple sacrifices, through the scholarship of the rabbis, to sedarim performed in many lands and ages, including ours tonight. We have considered the importance of our inner freedom—freedom from habit and freedom from prejudice. We have prayed for the world to be redeemed and reflected upon our responsibility to bring this about.

The focus of the Exodus story is the search for redemption and freedom. We end the Seder by returning to the spiritual heart of the Jew—represented by Jerusalem—and praying for a Messianic Age of justice and freedom for all.

A Selection of Songs

Va-Y'hi Ba-Chatzi Ha-Lailah

It came to pass at midnight.
Always Your wonders occurred in the night.
Before the first watch, at the start of the night,
Caught Abram the captors of Lot in the night.
  It came to pass at midnight.
Dreaming, Gerar's king heard Your judgment
at night, Even as Laban You warned in the night;
Fighting an angel, Israel won in the night.
  It came to pass at midnight.
Gone were the firstborn of Egypt at midnight;
Her offspring no more when they rose in the
night. Ill-luck the stars brought to Sisera
at night.
  It came to pass at midnight.
Judgment was swift on Assyria at night;
Knocked down was Babylon too in the night;
Light came to Daniel while dreaming at night.
  It came to pass at midnight.
Mad Belshazzar met his fate that same night;
Nought did the lions to Daniel at night;
On Haman recoiled the decree writ at night.
  It came to pass at midnight.
Persia's king You prevented from sleeping that
night. Redeem us when we ask: "What of the
night?" Say to us: "Morning comes after the
night."
  It came to pass at midnight.
Teach us to hope for the day without night;
Usher it in, for Yours are day and night;
Watch over Your City by day and by night;
Zion's God, vanquish the darkness of night.
  Let it come to pass at midnight.

לֶקֶט שִׁירִים
וַיְהִי בַּחֲצִי הַלַּיְלָה

וּבְכֵן, וַיְהִי בַּחֲצִי הַלַּיְלָה.
אָז רוֹב נִסִּים הִפְלֵאתָ בַּלַּיְלָה, בְּרֹאשׁ אַשְׁמוּרוֹת
זֶה הַלַּיְלָה, גֵּר־צֶדֶק נִצַּחְתּוֹ כְּנֶחֱלַק לוֹ לַיְלָה.
וַיְהִי בַּחֲצִי הַלַּיְלָה.
דַּנְתָּ מֶלֶךְ גְּרָר בַּחֲלוֹם הַלַּיְלָה, הִפְחַדְתָּ אֲרַמִּי
בְּאֶמֶשׁ לַיְלָה, וַיָּשַׂר יִשְׂרָאֵל לְמַלְאָךְ וַיּוּכַל־לוֹ
לַיְלָה.
וַיְהִי בַּחֲצִי הַלַּיְלָה.
זֶרַע בְּכוֹרֵי פַתְרוֹס מָחַצְתָּ בַּחֲצִי הַלַּיְלָה, חֵילָם
לֹא מָצְאוּ בְּקוּמָם בַּלַּיְלָה, טִיסַת נְגִיד חֲרֹשֶׁת
סִלִּיתָ בְּכוֹכְבֵי לַיְלָה.
וַיְהִי בַּחֲצִי הַלַּיְלָה.
יָעַץ מְחָרֵף לְנוֹפֵף אִוּוּי, הוֹבַשְׁתָּ פְגָרָיו בַּלַּיְלָה,
כָּרַע בֵּל וּמַצָּבוֹ בְּאִישׁוֹן־לַיְלָה, לְאִישׁ חֲמוּדוֹת
נִגְלָה רָז חֲזוֹת־לַיְלָה.
וַיְהִי בַּחֲצִי הַלַּיְלָה.
מִשְׁתַּכֵּר בִּכְלֵי־קֹדֶשׁ נֶהֱרַג בּוֹ בַּלַּיְלָה, נוֹשַׁע
מִבּוֹר־אֲרָיוֹת פּוֹתֵר בְּעִתּוּתֵי־לַיְלָה, שִׂנְאָה נָטַר
אֲגָגִי וְכָתַב סְפָרִים בַּלַּיְלָה.
וַיְהִי בַּחֲצִי הַלַּיְלָה.
עוֹרַרְתָּ נִצְחֲךָ עָלָיו בְּנֶדֶד שְׁנַת לַיְלָה, פּוּרָה
תִדְרוֹךְ לְשׁוֹמֵר מַה מִּלַּיְלָה, צָרַח כַּשּׁוֹמֵר וְשָׂח
אָתָא בֹקֶר וְגַם לַיְלָה.
וַיְהִי בַּחֲצִי הַלַּיְלָה.
קָרֵב יוֹם אֲשֶׁר הוּא לֹא יוֹם וְלֹא לַיְלָה, רָם
הוֹדַע כִּי־לְךָ הַיּוֹם אַף לְךָ הַלַּיְלָה, שׁוֹמְרִים
הַפְקֵד לְעִירְךָ כָּל־הַיּוֹם וְכָל־הַלַּיְלָה, תָּאִיר
כְּאוֹר־יוֹם חֶשְׁכַּת־לַיְלָה.
וַיְהִי בַּחֲצִי הַלַּיְלָה.

Jewish rabbinic tradition teaches that God's deliverance comes exactly at midnight, when suffering is at its darkest hour. Midnight is both the time of Israelite redemption and the death of the Egyptian firstborn. The rabbis emphasized that God was solely responsible for both because only God knows when it is exactly midnight.

KI LO NA-EH

To God praise belongs; to God praise is due.

Almighty in sovereignty, Beloved by right,
Your Chosen ones sing to You: Yours only, Yours
solely, Yours alone, Eternal One, is the realm.
To God praise belongs; to God praise is due.

Dominant in sovereignty, Excelling by right,
Your Faithful ones sing to You: Yours only, Yours
solely, Yours alone, Eternal One, is the realm.
To God praise belongs; to God praise is due.

Glorious in sovereignty, Hallowed by right,
Your Just ones sing to You: Yours only, Yours
solely, Yours alone, Eternal One, is the realm.
To God praise belongs; to God praise is due.

Kindly in sovereignty, Lawgiver by right, Your
Ministers sing to You: Yours only, Yours solely,
Yours alone, Eternal One, is the realm. To God
praise belongs; to God praise is due.

None like You in sovereignty, Omnipotent by
right, Your People sing to You: Yours only,
Yours solely, Yours alone, Eternal One, is the realm.
To God praise belongs; to God praise is due.

Resplendent in sovereignty, Sovereign by right,
Your Thankful ones sing to You: Yours only,
Yours solely, Yours alone, Eternal One, is the realm.
To God praise belongs; to God praise is due.

Unrivaled in sovereignty, Victorious by right,
Your Worshippers sing to You: Yours only, Yours
solely, Yours alone, Eternal One, is the realm.
To God praise belongs; to God praise is due.

Worthy of sovereignty, Wonderful by right,
Your Witnesses sing to You: Yours only, Yours
solely, Yours alone, Eternal One, is the realm.
To God praise belongs; to God praise is due.

כִּי לוֹ נָאֶה

כִּי לוֹ נָאֶה, כִּי לוֹ יָאֶה. אַדִּיר בִּמְלוּכָה, בָּחוּר
כַּהֲלָכָה, גְּדוּדָיו יֹאמְרוּ לוֹ: לְךָ וּלְךָ, לְךָ כִּי לְךָ, לְךָ
אַף לְךָ, לְךָ יְיָ הַמַּמְלָכָה. כִּי לוֹ נָאֶה, כִּי לוֹ יָאֶה.
דָּגוּל בִּמְלוּכָה, הָדוּר כַּהֲלָכָה, וָתִיקָיו יֹאמְרוּ
לוֹ: לְךָ וּלְךָ, לְךָ כִּי לְךָ, לְךָ אַף לְךָ, לְךָ יְיָ
הַמַּמְלָכָה. כִּי לוֹ נָאֶה, כִּי לוֹ יָאֶה.
זַכַּאי בִּמְלוּכָה, חָסִין כַּהֲלָכָה, טַפְסְרָיו יֹאמְרוּ
לוֹ: לְךָ וּלְךָ, לְךָ כִּי לְךָ, לְךָ אַף לְךָ, לְךָ יְיָ
הַמַּמְלָכָה. כִּי לוֹ נָאֶה, כִּי לוֹ יָאֶה.
יָחִיד בִּמְלוּכָה, כַּבִּיר כַּהֲלָכָה, לִמּוּדָיו יֹאמְרוּ
לוֹ: לְךָ וּלְךָ, לְךָ כִּי לְךָ, לְךָ אַף לְךָ, לְךָ יְיָ
הַמַּמְלָכָה. כִּי לוֹ נָאֶה, כִּי לוֹ יָאֶה.
מוֹשֵׁל בִּמְלוּכָה, נוֹרָא כַּהֲלָכָה, סְבִיבָיו יֹאמְרוּ
לוֹ: לְךָ וּלְךָ, לְךָ כִּי לְךָ, לְךָ אַף לְךָ, לְךָ יְיָ
הַמַּמְלָכָה. כִּי לוֹ נָאֶה, כִּי לוֹ יָאֶה.
עָנָו בִּמְלוּכָה, פּוֹדֶה כַּהֲלָכָה, צַדִּיקָיו יֹאמְרוּ
לוֹ: לְךָ וּלְךָ, לְךָ כִּי לְךָ, לְךָ אַף לְךָ, לְךָ יְיָ
הַמַּמְלָכָה. כִּי לוֹ נָאֶה, כִּי לוֹ יָאֶה.
קָדוֹשׁ בִּמְלוּכָה, רַחוּם כַּהֲלָכָה, שִׁנְאַנָּיו יֹאמְרוּ
לוֹ: לְךָ וּלְךָ, לְךָ כִּי לְךָ, לְךָ אַף לְךָ, לְךָ יְיָ
הַמַּמְלָכָה. כִּי לוֹ נָאֶה, כִּי לוֹ יָאֶה.
תַּקִּיף בִּמְלוּכָה, תּוֹמֵךְ כַּהֲלָכָה, תְּמִימָיו יֹאמְרוּ
לוֹ: לְךָ וּלְךָ, לְךָ כִּי לְךָ, לְךָ אַף לְךָ, לְךָ יְיָ
הַמַּמְלָכָה. כִּי לוֹ נָאֶה, כִּי לוֹ יָאֶה.

ADDIR HU

Mighty are You! May You rebuild Your house
soon, speedily, speedily, in our days soon! O
God, rebuild, O God, rebuild, rebuild Your
house soon!

Select are You, Grand are You, Distinguished
are You! May You rebuild Your house soon,
speedily, speedily, in our days soon! O God,
rebuild, O God, rebuild, rebuild Your house soon!

Glorious are You, Ancient are You, Just are
You! May You rebuild Your house soon, speedily,
speedily, in our days soon! O God, rebuild, O
God, rebuild, rebuild Your house soon!

אַדִּיר הוּא

אַדִּיר הוּא, יִבְנֶה בֵּיתוֹ בְּקָרוֹב. בִּמְהֵרָה,
בִּמְהֵרָה, בְּיָמֵינוּ בְּקָרוֹב. אֵל בְּנֵה, אֵל בְּנֵה, בְּנֵה
בֵיתְךָ בְּקָרוֹב.
בָּחוּר הוּא, גָּדוֹל הוּא, דָּגוּל הוּא, יִבְנֶה בֵּיתוֹ
בְּקָרוֹב. בִּמְהֵרָה, בִּמְהֵרָה, בְּיָמֵינוּ בְּקָרוֹב. אֵל
בְּנֵה, אֵל בְּנֵה, בְּנֵה בֵיתְךָ בְּקָרוֹב.
הָדוּר הוּא, וָתִיק הוּא, זַכַּאי הוּא, יִבְנֶה בֵּיתוֹ
בְּקָרוֹב. בִּמְהֵרָה, בִּמְהֵרָה, בְּיָמֵינוּ בְּקָרוֹב. אֵל
בְּנֵה, אֵל בְּנֵה, בְּנֵה בֵיתְךָ בְּקָרוֹב.

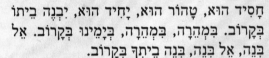

חָסִיד הוּא, טָהוֹר הוּא, יָחִיד הוּא, יִבְנֶה בֵּיתוֹ
בְּקָרוֹב. בִּמְהֵרָה, בִּמְהֵרָה, בְּיָמֵינוּ בְּקָרוֹב. אֵל
בְּנֵה, אֵל בְּנֵה, בְּנֵה בֵיתְךָ בְּקָרוֹב.
כַּבִּיר הוּא, לָמוּד הוּא, מֶלֶךְ הוּא, יִבְנֶה בֵּיתוֹ
בְּקָרוֹב. בִּמְהֵרָה, בִּמְהֵרָה, בְּיָמֵינוּ בְּקָרוֹב. אֵל
בְּנֵה, אֵל בְּנֵה, בְּנֵה בֵיתְךָ בְּקָרוֹב.
נוֹרָא הוּא, סַגִּיב הוּא, עִזּוּז הוּא, יִבְנֶה בֵּיתוֹ
בְּקָרוֹב. בִּמְהֵרָה, בִּמְהֵרָה, בְּיָמֵינוּ בְּקָרוֹב. אֵל
בְּנֵה, אֵל בְּנֵה, בְּנֵה בֵיתְךָ בְּקָרוֹב.
פּוֹדֶה הוּא, צַדִּיק הוּא, קָדוֹשׁ הוּא, יִבְנֶה בֵּיתוֹ
בְּקָרוֹב. בִּמְהֵרָה, בִּמְהֵרָה, בְּיָמֵינוּ בְּקָרוֹב. אֵל
בְּנֵה, אֵל בְּנֵה, בְּנֵה בֵיתְךָ בְּקָרוֹב.
רַחוּם הוּא, שַׁדַּי הוּא, תַּקִּיף הוּא, יִבְנֶה בֵּיתוֹ
בְּקָרוֹב. בִּמְהֵרָה, בִּמְהֵרָה, בְּיָמֵינוּ בְּקָרוֹב. אֵל
בְּנֵה, אֵל בְּנֵה, בְּנֵה בֵיתְךָ בְּקָרוֹב.

Pious are You, Unstained are You, Unique are You! May You rebuild Your house soon, speedily, speedily, in our days soon! O God, rebuild, O God, rebuild, rebuild Your house soon!

Strong are You, Wise are You, Sovereign are You! May You rebuild Your house soon, speedily, speedily, in our days soon! O God, rebuild, O God, rebuild, rebuild Your house soon!

Awesome are You, Exalted are You, Powerful are You! May You rebuild Your house soon, speedily, speedily, in our days soon! O God, rebuild, O God, rebuild, rebuild Your house soon!

Redeemer are You, Righteous are You, Holy are You! May You rebuild Your house soon, speedily, speedily, in our days soon! O God, rebuild, O God, rebuild, rebuild Your house soon!

Compassionate are You, Almighty are You, Powerful are You! May You rebuild Your house soon, speedily, speedily, in our days soon! O God, rebuild, O God, rebuild, rebuild Your house soon!

ECHAD MI YODEA

אֶחָד מִי יוֹדֵעַ

Who knows one? I know one: One is our God in heaven and on earth.

Who knows two? I know two: Two Tablets of the Law. One is our God in heaven and on earth.

Who knows three? I know three: Three Patriarchs. Two Tablets of the Law. One is our God in heaven and on earth.

Who knows four? I know four: Four Matriarchs. Three Patriarchs. Two Tablets of the Law. One is our God in heaven and on earth.

Who knows five? I know five: Five Books of Torah. Four Matriarchs. Three Patriarchs. Two Tablets of the Law. One is our God in heaven and on earth.

Who knows six? I know six: Six Orders of the Mishnah. Five Books of Torah. Four Matriarchs. Three Patriarchs. Two Tablets of the Law. One is our God in heaven and on earth.

אֶחָד מִי יוֹדֵעַ? אֶחָד אֲנִי יוֹדֵעַ. אֶחָד אֱלֹהֵינוּ
שֶׁבַּשָּׁמַיִם וּבָאָרֶץ.
שְׁנַיִם מִי יוֹדֵעַ? שְׁנַיִם אֲנִי יוֹדֵעַ. שְׁנֵי לֻחוֹת
הַבְּרִית. אֶחָד אֱלֹהֵינוּ שֶׁבַּשָּׁמַיִם וּבָאָרֶץ.
שְׁלֹשָׁה מִי יוֹדֵעַ? שְׁלֹשָׁה אֲנִי יוֹדֵעַ. שְׁלֹשָׁה
אָבוֹת. שְׁנֵי לֻחוֹת הַבְּרִית. אֶחָד אֱלֹהֵינוּ
שֶׁבַּשָּׁמַיִם וּבָאָרֶץ.
אַרְבַּע מִי יוֹדֵעַ? אַרְבַּע אֲנִי יוֹדֵעַ. אַרְבַּע
אִמָּהוֹת. שְׁלֹשָׁה אָבוֹת. שְׁנֵי לֻחוֹת הַבְּרִית.
אֶחָד אֱלֹהֵינוּ שֶׁבַּשָּׁמַיִם וּבָאָרֶץ.
חֲמִשָּׁה מִי יוֹדֵעַ? חֲמִשָּׁה אֲנִי יוֹדֵעַ. חֲמִשָּׁה
חֻמְשֵׁי תוֹרָה. אַרְבַּע אִמָּהוֹת. שְׁלֹשָׁה אָבוֹת.
שְׁנֵי לֻחוֹת הַבְּרִית. אֶחָד אֱלֹהֵינוּ שֶׁבַּשָּׁמַיִם
וּבָאָרֶץ.
שִׁשָּׁה מִי יוֹדֵעַ? שִׁשָּׁה אֲנִי יוֹדֵעַ. שִׁשָּׁה סִדְרֵי
מִשְׁנָה. חֲמִשָּׁה חֻמְשֵׁי תוֹרָה. אַרְבַּע אִמָּהוֹת.
שְׁלֹשָׁה אָבוֹת. שְׁנֵי לֻחוֹת הַבְּרִית. אֶחָד אֱלֹהֵינוּ
שֶׁבַּשָּׁמַיִם וּבָאָרֶץ.

Who knows seven? I know seven: Seven Days of the Week. Six Orders of the Mishnah. Five Books of Torah. Four Matriarchs. Three Patriarchs. Two Tablets of the Law. One is our God in heaven and on earth.

Who knows eight? I know eight: Eight Days to Circumcision. Seven Days of the Week. Six Orders of the Mishnah. Five Books of Torah. Four Matriarchs. Three Patriarchs. Two Tablets of the Law. One is our God in heaven and on earth.

Who knows nine? I know nine: Nine Months to Childbirth. Eight Days to Circumcision. Seven Days of the Week. Six Orders of the Mishnah. Five Books of Torah. Four Matriarchs. Three Patriarchs. Two Tablets of the Law. One is our God in heaven and on earth.

Who knows ten? I know ten: Ten Commandments. Nine Months to Childbirth. Eight Days to Circumcision. Seven Days of the Week. Six Orders of the Mishnah. Five Books of Torah. Four Matriarchs. Three Patriarchs. Two Tablets of the Law. One is our God in heaven and on earth.

Who knows eleven? I know eleven: Eleven Stars in Joseph's dream. Ten Commandments. Nine Months to Childbirth. Eight Days to Circumcision. Seven Days of the Week. Six Orders of the Mishnah. Five Books of Torah. Four Matriarchs. Three Patriarchs. Two Tablets of the Law. One is our God in heaven and on earth.

Who knows twelve? I know twelve: Twelve Tribes of Israel. Eleven Stars in Joseph's dream. Ten Commandments. Nine Months to Childbirth. Eight Days to Circumcision. Seven Days of the Week. Six Orders of the Mishnah. Five Books of Torah. Four Matriarchs. Three Patriarchs. Two Tablets of the Law. One is our God in heaven and on earth.

Who knows thirteen? I know thirteen: Thirteen Attributes of God. Twelve Tribes of Israel. Eleven Stars in Joseph's dream. Ten Commandments. Nine Months to Childbirth. Eight Days to Circumcision. Seven Days of the Week. Six Orders of the Mishnah. Five Books of Torah. Four Matriarchs. Three Patriarchs. Two Tablets of the Law. One is our God in heaven and on earth.

שִׁבְעָה מִי יוֹדֵעַ? שִׁבְעָה אֲנִי יוֹדֵעַ. שִׁבְעָה יְמֵי שַׁבַּתָּא. שִׁשָּׁה סִדְרֵי מִשְׁנָה. חֲמִשָּׁה חֻמְשֵׁי תוֹרָה. אַרְבַּע אִמָּהוֹת. שְׁלֹשָׁה אָבוֹת. שְׁנֵי לֻחוֹת הַבְּרִית. אֶחָד אֱלֹהֵינוּ שֶׁבַּשָּׁמַיִם וּבָאָרֶץ.

שְׁמוֹנָה מִי יוֹדֵעַ? שְׁמוֹנָה אֲנִי יוֹדֵעַ. שְׁמוֹנָה יְמֵי מִילָה. שִׁבְעָה יְמֵי שַׁבַּתָּא. שִׁשָּׁה סִדְרֵי מִשְׁנָה. חֲמִשָּׁה חֻמְשֵׁי תוֹרָה. אַרְבַּע אִמָּהוֹת. שְׁלֹשָׁה אָבוֹת. שְׁנֵי לֻחוֹת הַבְּרִית. אֶחָד אֱלֹהֵינוּ שֶׁבַּשָּׁמַיִם וּבָאָרֶץ.

תִּשְׁעָה מִי יוֹדֵעַ? תִּשְׁעָה אֲנִי יוֹדֵעַ. תִּשְׁעָה יַרְחֵי לֵדָה. שְׁמוֹנָה יְמֵי מִילָה. שִׁבְעָה יְמֵי שַׁבַּתָּא. שִׁשָּׁה סִדְרֵי מִשְׁנָה. חֲמִשָּׁה חֻמְשֵׁי תוֹרָה. אַרְבַּע אִמָּהוֹת. שְׁלֹשָׁה אָבוֹת. שְׁנֵי לֻחוֹת הַבְּרִית. אֶחָד אֱלֹהֵינוּ שֶׁבַּשָּׁמַיִם וּבָאָרֶץ.

עֲשָׂרָה מִי יוֹדֵעַ? עֲשָׂרָה אֲנִי יוֹדֵעַ. עֲשָׂרָה דִבְּרַיָּא. תִּשְׁעָה יַרְחֵי לֵדָה. שְׁמוֹנָה יְמֵי מִילָה. שִׁבְעָה יְמֵי שַׁבַּתָּא. שִׁשָּׁה סִדְרֵי מִשְׁנָה. חֲמִשָּׁה חֻמְשֵׁי תוֹרָה. אַרְבַּע אִמָּהוֹת. שְׁלֹשָׁה אָבוֹת. שְׁנֵי לֻחוֹת הַבְּרִית. אֶחָד אֱלֹהֵינוּ שֶׁבַּשָּׁמַיִם וּבָאָרֶץ.

אַחַד עָשָׂר מִי יוֹדֵעַ? אַחַד עָשָׂר אֲנִי יוֹדֵעַ. אַחַד עָשָׂר כּוֹכְבַיָּא. עֲשָׂרָה דִבְּרַיָּא. תִּשְׁעָה יַרְחֵי לֵדָה. שְׁמוֹנָה יְמֵי מִילָה. שִׁבְעָה יְמֵי שַׁבַּתָּא. שִׁשָּׁה סִדְרֵי מִשְׁנָה. חֲמִשָּׁה חֻמְשֵׁי תוֹרָה. אַרְבַּע אִמָּהוֹת. שְׁלֹשָׁה אָבוֹת. שְׁנֵי לֻחוֹת הַבְּרִית. אֶחָד אֱלֹהֵינוּ שֶׁבַּשָּׁמַיִם וּבָאָרֶץ.

שְׁנֵים עָשָׂר מִי יוֹדֵעַ? שְׁנֵים עָשָׂר אֲנִי יוֹדֵעַ. שְׁנֵים עָשָׂר שִׁבְטַיָּא. אַחַד עָשָׂר כּוֹכְבַיָּא. עֲשָׂרָה דִבְּרַיָּא. תִּשְׁעָה יַרְחֵי לֵדָה. שְׁמוֹנָה יְמֵי מִילָה. שִׁבְעָה יְמֵי שַׁבַּתָּא. שִׁשָּׁה סִדְרֵי מִשְׁנָה. חֲמִשָּׁה חֻמְשֵׁי תוֹרָה. אַרְבַּע אִמָּהוֹת. שְׁלֹשָׁה אָבוֹת. שְׁנֵי לֻחוֹת הַבְּרִית. אֶחָד אֱלֹהֵינוּ שֶׁבַּשָּׁמַיִם וּבָאָרֶץ.

שְׁלֹשָׁה עָשָׂר מִי יוֹדֵעַ? שְׁלֹשָׁה עָשָׂר אֲנִי יוֹדֵעַ. שְׁלֹשָׁה עָשָׂר מִדַּיָּא. שְׁנֵים עָשָׂר שִׁבְטַיָּא. אַחַד עָשָׂר כּוֹכְבַיָּא. עֲשָׂרָה דִבְּרַיָּא. תִּשְׁעָה יַרְחֵי לֵדָה. שְׁמוֹנָה יְמֵי מִילָה. שִׁבְעָה יְמֵי שַׁבַּתָּא. שִׁשָּׁה סִדְרֵי מִשְׁנָה. חֲמִשָּׁה חֻמְשֵׁי תוֹרָה. אַרְבַּע אִמָּהוֹת. שְׁלֹשָׁה אָבוֹת. שְׁנֵי לֻחוֹת הַבְּרִית. אֶחָד אֱלֹהֵינוּ שֶׁבַּשָּׁמַיִם וּבָאָרֶץ.

CHAD GADYA

One kid, one kid my father bought for two zuzim: one kid, one kid.

Then came a cat and ate the kid my father bought for two zuzim: one kid, one kid.

Then came a dog and bit the cat that ate the kid my father bought for two zuzim: one kid, one kid.

Then came a stick and beat the dog that bit the cat that ate the kid my father bought for two zuzim: one kid, one kid.

Then fire came and burned the stick that beat the dog that bit the cat that ate the kid my father bought for two zuzim: one kid, one kid.

Then water came and quenched the fire that burned the stick that beat the dog that bit the cat that ate the kid my father bought for two zuzim: one kid, one kid.

Then came an ox and drank the water that quenched the fire that burned the stick that beat the dog that bit the cat that ate the kid my father bought for two zuzim: one kid, one kid.

Then came a butcher and slew the ox that drank the water that quenched the fire that burned the stick that beat the dog that bit the cat that ate the kid my father bought for two zuzim: one kid, one kid.

Then came the Angel of Death and slew the butcher that slew the ox that drank the water that quenched the fire that burned the stick that beat the dog that bit the cat that ate the kid my father bought for two zuzim: one kid, one kid.

Then came the Holy One, ever to be blessed, and slew the Angel of Death that slew the butcher that slew the ox that drank the water that quenched the fire that burned the stick that beat the dog that bit the cat that ate the kid my father bought for two zuzim: one kid, one kid.

חַד גַּדְיָא

חַד גַּדְיָא, חַד גַּדְיָא דְּזַבֵּן אַבָּא בִּתְרֵי זוּזֵי: חַד גַּדְיָא, חַד גַּדְיָא.

וְאָתָא שֻׁנְרָא וְאָכְלָה לְגַדְיָא דְּזַבֵּן אַבָּא בִּתְרֵי זוּזֵי: חַד גַּדְיָא, חַד גַּדְיָא.

וְאָתָא כַלְבָּא וְנָשַׁךְ לְשֻׁנְרָא דְּאָכְלָה לְגַדְיָא דְּזַבֵּן אַבָּא בִּתְרֵי זוּזֵי: חַד גַּדְיָא, חַד גַּדְיָא.

וְאָתָא חוּטְרָא וְהִכָּה לְכַלְבָּא דְּנָשַׁךְ לְשֻׁנְרָא דְּאָכְלָה לְגַדְיָא דְּזַבֵּן אַבָּא בִּתְרֵי זוּזֵי: חַד גַּדְיָא, חַד גַּדְיָא.

וְאָתָא נוּרָא וְשָׂרַף לְחוּטְרָא דְּהִכָּה לְכַלְבָּא דְּנָשַׁךְ לְשֻׁנְרָא דְּאָכְלָה לְגַדְיָא דְּזַבֵּן אַבָּא בִּתְרֵי זוּזֵי: חַד גַּדְיָא, חַד גַּדְיָא.

וְאָתָא מַיָּא וְכָבָה לְנוּרָא דְּשָׂרַף לְחוּטְרָא דְּהִכָּה לְכַלְבָּא דְּנָשַׁךְ לְשֻׁנְרָא דְּאָכְלָה לְגַדְיָא דְּזַבֵּן אַבָּא בִּתְרֵי זוּזֵי: חַד גַּדְיָא, חַד גַּדְיָא.

וְאָתָא תוֹרָא וְשָׁתָא לְמַיָּא דְּכָבָה לְנוּרָא דְּשָׂרַף לְחוּטְרָא דְּהִכָּה לְכַלְבָּא דְּנָשַׁךְ לְשֻׁנְרָא דְּאָכְלָה לְגַדְיָא דְּזַבֵּן אַבָּא בִּתְרֵי זוּזֵי: חַד גַּדְיָא, חַד גַּדְיָא.

וְאָתָא הַשּׁוֹחֵט וְשָׁחַט לְתוֹרָא דְּשָׁתָא לְמַיָּא דְּכָבָה לְנוּרָא דְּשָׂרַף לְחוּטְרָא דְּהִכָּה לְכַלְבָּא דְּנָשַׁךְ לְשֻׁנְרָא דְּאָכְלָה לְגַדְיָא דְּזַבֵּן אַבָּא בִּתְרֵי זוּזֵי: חַד גַּדְיָא, חַד גַּדְיָא.

וְאָתָא מַלְאַךְ הַמָּוֶת וְשָׁחַט לְשׁוֹחֵט דְּשָׁחַט לְתוֹרָא דְּשָׁתָא לְמַיָּא דְּכָבָה לְנוּרָא דְּשָׂרַף לְחוּטְרָא דְּהִכָּה לְכַלְבָּא דְּנָשַׁךְ לְשֻׁנְרָא דְּאָכְלָה לְגַדְיָא דְּזַבֵּן אַבָּא בִּתְרֵי זוּזֵי: חַד גַּדְיָא, חַד גַּדְיָא.

וְאָתָא הַקָּדוֹשׁ בָּרוּךְ הוּא וְשָׁחַט לְמַלְאַךְ הַמָּוֶת דְּשָׁחַט לְשׁוֹחֵט דְּשָׁחַט לְתוֹרָא דְּשָׁתָא לְמַיָּא דְּכָבָה לְנוּרָא דְּשָׂרַף לְחוּטְרָא דְּהִכָּה לְכַלְבָּא דְּנָשַׁךְ לְשֻׁנְרָא דְּאָכְלָה לְגַדְיָא דְּזַבֵּן אַבָּא בִּתְרֵי זוּזֵי: חַד גַּדְיָא, חַד גַּדְיָא.

This song became part of the Haggadah after the 15th century, although it is written in Aramaic, the language spoken by the Jews in the 1st century. It is an allegory in which the characters symbolize events in Jewish history. Israel is the "kid" that God bought for two zuzim, the tablets of the Ten Commandments. Then Israel suffers at the hands of foreign powers, each one destroying its predecessor: the cat is Assyria, the dog is Babylonia, the stick is Persia, the fire is Macedonia, the water is Rome, the ox is the Saracens, the butcher is the Crusaders, and the Angel of Death is the Turkish Empire. It is a song of survival: Though we have suffered generations of persecution, today we flourish as a vibrant community.

COUNTING THE OMER

סְפִירַת הָעוֹמֶר

(recited only on the second night)

Blessed are You, our Eternal God, Ruler of the universe whose mitzvot add holiness to our lives and who gave us the mitzvah of counting the Omer.

בָּרוּךְ אַתָּה יְיָ, אֱלֹהֵינוּ מֶלֶךְ הָעוֹלָם, אֲשֶׁר קִדְּשָׁנוּ בְּמִצְוֹתָיו וְצִוָּנוּ עַל סְפִירַת הָעוֹמֶר.

Today is the first day of the Omer.

הַיּוֹם יוֹם אֶחָד לָעוֹמֶר.

Although the Israelites were liberated from Egypt, as they journeyed through the wilderness they longed for their uncomplicated life of captivity. It was only when they arrived at Mount Sinai and received the Ten Commandments that they became truly free—free to create a new society with a framework of just laws in a promised land.

This period of 49 days from the Exodus—celebrated by Pesach—to the giving of the Ten Commandments—celebrated by the festival of Shavuot—is known as the Omer. The name comes from ancient times when an offering of one measure (omer) of barley from the harvest was brought to the Temple every day, from Pesach until Shavuot. After the Temple was destroyed, the tradition developed of counting the days of this period, a tradition still alive today. Counting each day symbolizes each step taken from Egypt to Mount Sinai, from oppression to freedom.

During the Middle Ages, the Omer became associated with sadness and mourning, when the solemnization of marriages was prohibited, a custom still observed today.

INDEX OF MANUSCRIPTS

The following manuscripts are featured in this Haggadah:

Hispano-Moresque Haggadah *(Sephardic)*
BL MS Or. 2737, Castile, ca. 1300
Vellum, 160 x 120 mm
The *Hispano-Moresque Haggadah* includes 66 full-page illuminations, showing scenes from the book of Exodus, the Binding of Isaac, and Passover rituals. A combination of Italianate and archaistic styles is evident in the miniatures, as well as in the decorated initial-word panels in the text. The illuminations, executed in bright and pastel color washes and colored inks, are probably the work of two artists from the same workshop as there are differences in the composition of scenes and the rendering of human figures. The lack of a colophon (which most Spanish Haggadah manuscripts have) makes it difficult to identify who the artists were and exactly when and where the manuscript was produced.

Brother Haggadah *(Sephardic)*
BL MS Or. 1404, Catalonia, 14th century
Vellum, 273 x 234 mm
The iconography and decoration of the *Brother Haggadah* are similar to those of the *Rylands Haggadah* (Rylands Library, Manchester), hence its name—it is likely that the artists of both haggadot used a common model. The *Brother Haggadah* is also known as the *Shealtiel Haggadah*, due to the inscription on folio 50v indicating the name of one of its owners.

The manuscript includes 13 full-page panels, each divided into two sections. The biblical miniatures show scenes from the book of Exodus. The decoration includes ritual representations and textual illustrations as well as initial-word panels. The artist used a combination of several stylistic elements: the decorated word panels suggest French influence while the human figures and architectural components are Italian in style. The miniatures were painted with heavy gouache paints. Burnished gold was used to decorate the word panels.

Golden Haggadah *(Sephardic)*
BL MS Add. 27210, Barcelona ca. 1320
Vellum, 247 x 198 mm
The *Golden Haggadah* is undoubtedly one of the most beautiful, lavish Spanish illuminated Haggadah manuscripts. Its earliest known owner was Rabbi Joav Gallico of Asti (near Turin) who gave it to his daughter Rosa and her husband Eliah as a wedding gift in 1602. (Some scholars believe that it was brought to Italy around 1492 by Jews expelled from Spain.) The manuscript belonged to the famous bibliophile, Joseph Almanzi of Padua, during the 19th century—we do not know how it came into his hands. The fame of the manuscript and its name come from the 14 full-page miniatures, each divided into four panels with a tooled gold leaf background. The illuminations contain 71 episodes based on Genesis, Exodus, and Midrashic stories, and some Passover ritual scenes. There are also decorative initial-word panels and titles, some with zoomorphic motifs. Two artists belonging to the same workshop were responsible for the illuminations: some of the miniatures are better balanced than

others, with graceful and elegant figures indicating the work of a more skilled artist. French-Gothic and Italo-Byzantine influences are apparent in the full-page illuminations, whereas the geometric patterns found in several of the textual illustrations and the zoomorphic letters reveal Eastern and archaistic stylistic influences respectively.

Sister Haggadah *(Sephardic)*
BL MS Or. 2884, Barcelona, mid-14th century
Parchment, 230 x 190 mm
There are many similarities between the iconography in the *Golden Haggadah* and the iconography in this manuscript, hence its name. According to some scholars, the artists of both manuscripts based their work on a common model. The *Sister Haggadah* has 34 full-page panels illustrating 86 scenes from Genesis and Exodus, and some ritual and textual illustrations. As in the *Golden Haggadah*, a combination of French-Gothic, Italian, and archaistic styles shows in the decoration, although the artistry is not as skilled.

Ashkenazi Haggadah *(Ashkenazic)*
BL MS Add. 14762, North Italy and Germany, ca. 1460-1475
Vellum, 375 x 280 mm
The *Ashkenazi Haggadah* is one of the most exquisite German medieval haggadot. As well as relating the story of the Exodus, written in beautiful calligraphy, it contains a commentary (attributed to Eleazar ben Judah of Worms) in cursive script, ritual and textual illuminations, and handsomely adorned initial-letter and -word panels.

The colophon on folio 48b indicates that the manuscript was illustrated by Joel ben Simeon Feibusch for the patron Jacob Mattathias. No date or location is given. Joel ben Simeon was probably born in Cologne in the early 1420s and moved to Bonn at an early age with his family. There he received his initial training as a scribe-artist. He spent some of his life in Northern Italy, where he may have been known as the "Ashkenazi" because of his German origins—hence the name *Ashkenazi Haggadah*.

As the manuscript displays a combination of Italianate and German styles of illumination, some scholars argue that Joel ben Simeon was the sole illustrator. Despite the colophon, other scholars maintain that two different artists were responsible for the illuminations: Joel ben Simeon for the delicate, slender Italianate figures and the motifs, and a second artist, identified as Johannes Bämler of Augsburg, for the stouter, heavily clad figures as well as the richly colored, gold-embossed initial-word panels. Another theory is that the work was executed by various artists and scribes in Joel ben Simeon's workshop.

Barcelona Haggadah *(Sephardic)*
BL MS Add. 14761, Barcelona, mid- to late 14th century
Vellum, 255 x 190 mm
Unlike other Spanish haggadot, the *Barcelona Haggadah* does not feature the typical cycle of full-page biblical illustrations preceding the text of the Passover story. Nearly all of its folios contain decorations and illustrations of Passover rituals and

biblical and Midrashic scenes referred to in the text. The initial-word panels, particularly those with extending foliage scrolls framing the text, are very striking.

The illustrations and decorations display elements from Italian and French schools of illumination. Human figures, hybrids, and animals are interwoven with flowers and leaves as decoration, and sometimes animals rather than humans are shown performing various rituals, a humorous approach probably borrowed from Latin codices. The illustrations are a valuable source of information on Jewish costume, ritual, and musical life in medieval Spain, before the expulsion of 1492.

There is no colophon, but most scholars believe that the manuscript was produced in or near Barcelona. Some interpret the four azure-and-gold striped coats of arms on folio 61r (page 33) as the 14th-century heraldic device of Barcelona. Others see the coats of arms as decorative motifs and make the connection with Barcelona on grounds of the manuscript's style. The costumes and decorative motifs indicate that the manuscript was probably executed in the last half of the 14th century.

Notes:

(Front and back cover) BL MS Add. 14761, f.59v (detail) *(Barcelona Hagg.)*
According to Dr. Evelyn Cohen, this is an "historiated initial-word panel" placed at the beginning of an important statement made by Rabbi Gamaliel: in order to fulfil your obligation at Passover, you must discuss the meanings of Pesach, Matzah, and Maror. The image shows the Rabbi instructing four students.

(pp. 2–3, 63) BL MS Or. 2737, f. 1r *(Hispano-Moresque Hagg.)*
This miniature of a vine tree with leaves, sprigs, and grape clusters, figures on the frontispiece of the *Hispano-Moresque Haggadah*, and may be a symbolic reminder of the Four Cups of wine. The vine is also associated with peace and hope—feelings shared by all who celebrate Passover.

(p. 5) BL MS Or. 2884, f. 18r *(Sister Hagg.)*
The family Seder. The miniature, painted in an Italianate style, conveys the festive and dignified atmosphere of the occasion.

(pp. 6–7) BL MS Add. 14762, f. 39r (detail) *(Ashkenazi Hagg.)*
Decoration from panel with the first word of "Nishmat kol hai" ("The soul of every living being").

(p. 8) BL MS Add. 14762, f.1v *(Ashkenazi Hagg.)*
The search for leaven on the night before Passover using feathers and a candle. The Hebrew word "Or" ("Light") in the panel refers to the custom of searching by candle light.

(p. 9) BL MS Add. 14761, f.20v (detail) *(Barcelona Hagg.)*
The Hebrew word in the panel is "Va-yikah" ("And he takes") referring to the matzah which the father is holding.

(p. 10) BL MS Add. 14762, f. 4v (detail) *(Ashkenazi Hagg.)*
Panel containing the word "Baruch" ("Blessed") before the Sanctification and the First Cup.

(p. 11) BL MS Add. 14761, f. 26v (detail) *(Barcelona Hagg.)*
Panel containing the word "Baruch" ("Blessed") before Havdalah.

(p. 12) BL MS Add. 14761, f. 19v (detail) *(Barcelona Hagg.)*
The First Cup; the panel contains the word "Ve-shotin" ("And they drink").

(p. 13) BL MS Add. 14761, f. 19v (detail) *(Barcelona Hagg.)*
The ritual of washing the hands.

(p. 14) BL MS Add. 14762, f. 6v *(Ashkenazi Hagg.)*
The Second Cup is filled and a panel containing the first word, "Mah" ("Why"), of the Mah Nishtanah. The Mah Nishtanah is rarely illustrated but is more likely to be found illustrated in Ashkenazic haggadot.

(p. 15) BL MS Add. 14761, f. 43r (detail) *(Barcelona Hagg.)*
The labor of the Israelites.

(p. 16) BL MS Add. 14762, f. 7v (detail) *(Ashkenazi Hagg.)*
The Five Rabbis of B'nei B'rak discussing the Passover story.

(p. 17) BL MS Add. 14761, f. 32v (detail) *(Barcelona Hagg.)*
Panel containing the words "Amar El'azar" referring to El'azar ben Azariah.

(p. 18) BL MS Add. 14762, f. 9v (detail) *(Ashkenazi Hagg.)*
The upper figure represents the simple child; the lower figure represents the child who does not know how to ask. According to some scholars, in Ashkenazic haggadot the simple child is usually portrayed as a jester.

(p. 19) BL MS Add. 14762, f. 9r *(Ashkenazi Hagg.)*
In both Ashkenazic and Sephardic haggadot, the wicked son is traditionally represented as a soldier. Here, he is dressed in armor and strikes a child who is wearing a yellow badge. This may be a comment on the social condition of Jews during the Middle Ages. The Church obliged them to wear yellow badges to distinguish them from Christians. The badge was introduced in Italy in the 13th century and in Germany in the 15th century.

(p. 20) BL MS Add. 14762, f. 11v (detail) *(Ashkenazi Hagg.)*
The figure represents a wandering Aramean, probably Jacob.

(p. 21) BL MS Add. 14762, f.12r (detail) *(Ashkenazi Hagg.)*
A strutting cock whose body contains a portion of commentary.

(pp. 22–23) BL MS Add. 14762, f. 14v and f. 15r (detail) *(Ashkenazi Hagg.)*
The Israelites flee Egypt, pursued by the Egyptian army. The two groups are separated by a blue pillar of cloud which, according to the Midrash, protected the Israelites from the Egyptians' arrows. Moses carries his staff and he follows the pillar of fire, leading the Israelites towards the sea. He looks up towards the divine hand appearing through a blue cloud, an allusion to "...a strong hand and an outstretched arm" with which God delivered the Israelites.

(p. 24) BL MS Add. 14762, f.13v (detail) *(Ashkenazi Hagg.)*
Two decorative panels containing the letter "Vav" ("and", which begins each commentary), adorned with animal and floral motifs.

(p. 25) BL MS Add. 14762, f.14r (detail) *(Ashkenazi Hagg.)*
The upper image depicts a crowned figure, possibly Pharaoh; the lower image depicts a stag with his foot caught in a dog's mouth which, according to Dr. D. Goldstein, may be a symbol of the Israelites' captivity.

(p. 26) BL MS Add. 27210, f. 12v *(Golden Hagg.)*
The panels illustrate the plagues of frogs, lice, wild beasts, and cattle disease. Italian influences are evident in the architectural features.

(p. 27) BL MS Add. 14762, f. 17r *(Ashkenazi Hagg.)*
The Ten Plagues. (See commentary on page 27.)

(pp. 28–29) BL MS Or. 1404, f.16r *(Brother Hagg.)*
(See commentary on page 29.) The earliest use of repeated words as decoration in conjunction with the Dayenu was found in a fragment of an 11th-century Haggadah from the Cairo Genizah in Egypt.

(p. 30) BL MS Or. 2737, f.20v (detail) *(Hispano-Moresque Hagg.)*
Rabbi Gamaliel and his students.

(p. 31) BL MS Add. 14761, f. 60r (detail) *(Barcelona Hagg.)*
A person roasts a lamb on a spit in the panel which contains the word "Pesach." Professor Bezalel Narkiss refers to this as an "historiated initial word panel" as it is a clear reminder of the custom of roasting the lamb before the destruction of the Second Temple.

(p. 32) BL MS Add. 14762 f. 22r *(Ashkenazi Hagg.)*
The decorated Hebrew word spells "Matzah." Most Haggadah manuscripts have illustrations of matzah and maror which some scholars regard as the oldest illustrations to the Haggadah text. As in this illustration, it is common in Ashkenazic and Italian haggadot to depict the matzah being held by a man. The figure is representative of Joel Ben Simeon's style seen in his other manuscripts.

(p. 33) BL MS Add. 14761, f. 61r *(Barcelona Hagg.)*
This elaborate full-page illustration has often been cited in discussions about the manuscript's origins. The matzah, placed in a square frame, is shown as a roundel decorated with eight shields. At each of the four corners, there is a trumpeter, probably representing the Four Winds. According to some scholars, the musicians are sounding the harmony of the universe, represented by the matzah.

(p. 34) BL MS Add. 14762, f.22v *(Ashkenazi Hagg.)*
The decorated Hebrew word spells "Maror."

(p. 35) BL MS Or. 1404, f.18r *(Brother Hagg.)*
The husband featured on the left-hand side of the lower register points to his wife. According to Professor Bezalel Narkiss, this jocular gesture was common at this point in the Seder in many Jewish communities during the Middle Ages. The sticks in the two cups on the Seder table are celery stalks, often used in Sephardic communities as maror.

(p. 36) BL MS Add. 14762, f. 45r (detail) *(Ashkenazi Hagg.)*
The upper figure is a bearded man wearing a yellow badge; below is a floral adornment with radiating gold dots.

(p. 37) BL MS Add. 14761, f.65v (detail) *(Barcelona Hagg.)*
Miniature illustrating a synagogue and containing the word "Hallelujah." The cantor holds up a Torah scroll in a decorated round case like those used in Sephardic communities.

(p. 39) BL MS Add. 14762, f. 6r (detail) *(Ashkenazi Hagg.)*
The Passover Seder.

(p. 40) BL MS Add. 14761, f. 28r (detail) *(Barcelona Hagg.)*
Finding the Afikoman.

(p. 41) BL MS Add. 14761, f. 25r (detail) *(Barcelona Hagg.)*
Marginal decoration with human, floral, and animal motifs.

(pp. 42–43) BL MS Add. 14761, f. 22v (detail) *(Barcelona Hagg.)*
Elaborate decorative borders with acanthus leaves and acorns, displaying peacocks.

(p. 44) BL MS Add. 14761, f. 31v (detail) *(Barcelona Hagg.)*
Intricately adorned borders consisting of foliage scrolls with animals, birds, and grotesques.

(p. 45) BL MS Add. 27210, f.83r (detail) *(Golden Hagg.)*
Gold leaf panel with geometric designs forming a six-pointed star, with palmette and ivy scrolls.

(p. 46) BL MS Add. 14761, f. 71v (detail) *(Barcelona Hagg.)*
Elaborate panel containing "Shefokh," the first word of "Pour out thy wrath." At this point in Ashkenazic manuscripts there is sometimes an illustration of a house or a building with the door opened for Elijah, the prophet (or the Messiah), riding a white ass. This messianic motif is absent in Sephardic haggadot, in which the imagery is often a literal interpretation of the verse "Pour out thy wrath," as shown here. The angel pours a cup, a reminder of the Fourth Cup at this point in the Seder.

(p. 47) BL MS Add. 27210, f. 47r *(Golden Hagg.)*
Word panel with extended adornments and golden letters spelling "Hallelujah."

(p. 48) BL MS Add. 14762, f. 35r *(Ashkenazi Hagg.)*
Panel with first word of "Min ha-metsar karati Yah" ("In distress I called upon the Eternal").

(p. 49) BL MS Add. 14762, f. 37v *(Ashkenazi Hagg.)*
Panel with the first word of "Hodu la-Adonai ki tov" ("Give thanks to the Eternal").

(p. 50) BL MS Add. 14762, f. 39r *(Ashkenazi Hagg.)*
Panel with the first word of "Nishmat kol hai" ("The soul of every living being").

(p. 52) BL MS Add. 14761, f. 55v (detail) *(Barcelona Hagg.)*
Marginal decoration of a dragon with its tail extending as foliage.

(p. 53) BL MS Add. 14761, f. 88r *(Barcelona Hagg.)*
This miniature illustrating "Next year in Jerusalem" is an exception, as the verse is rarely illustrated in Sephardic haggadot. In Ashkenazic manuscripts, the verse is often illustrated as the city of Jerusalem or the Temple, and sometimes both.

(p. 54) BL MS Add. 27210, f. 78v (detail) *(Golden Hagg.)*
Vertical decoration in blue and magenta with upper and lower ivy scrolls.

(p. 55) BL MS Add. 27210, f. 62r (detail) *(Golden Hagg.)*
Horizontal decoration with parallel scrolls emerging from a golden palmette.

(p. 56) BL MS Add. 27210, f. 78v (detail) *(Golden Hagg.)*
Vertical, golden decoration with buds.

(p. 57) BL MS Add. 27210, f. 73r *(Golden Hagg.)*
Vertical decoration in blue, magenta, and green with scrolls extending from parallel cusps.

(p. 58) BL MS Add. 27210, f. 68r (detail) *(Golden Hagg.)*
Decorative bar with palmette, symmetrical foliage, and dragon.

(p. 59) BL MS Add. 27210, f. 24r *(Golden Hagg.)*
Golden frame decorated with a pattern of leaves and red berries.

• *Index compiled by Ilana Tahan, Curator of the Hebrew Section of the British Library.*